# The Trust Transformation

The Final Transformation

"Powerful, useful wisdom. When in doubt, wear the bracelet. Especially then."
—**Seth Godin,** author, *This is Marketing*

"Those who lead - and those who research and practice leadership - all agree that "trust" is the basic building block of positive personal interactions and critical engagements. This study by Mansfield and Reid provides the intricacies of the dynamics, application, and principles of the concept of trust, making this book a must-read for those who want to lead."
—**Mark Hertling,** Lieutenant General, US Army (retired), Author, *Growing Physician Leaders*

"Leading in healthcare today is only as effective as the foundational trust that is created with those you lead. Engagement, influence, relationships, and change all begin with fundamental trust. This study, *The Trust Transformation,* is a guide to help build that kind of trust. A must read for all leaders."
—**Michael Cacciatore, MD,** Chief Clinical Officer, AdventHealth

# THE
# TRUST
# TRANSFORMATION

*Transform Your*
**Health, Wellbeing, and Performance**
*Through the Power of Trust*

# ROY REID &
# OMAYRA MANSFIELD, MD

NEW YORK

LONDON • NASHVILLE • MELBOURNE • VANCOUVER

# The Trust Transformation

Transform Your Health, Wellbeing, and Performance Through the Power of Trust

Published in New York, New York, by Morgan James Publishing. Morgan James is a trademark of Morgan James, LLC. www.MorganJamesPublishing.com

Proudly distributed by Publishers Group West®

Unless Otherwise Marked, All Are Scriptures are From the Holy Bible, New International Version®, NIV® Copyright © 1973, 1978, 1984, 2011 by Biblica, Inc.™ Used by permission of Zondervan

**A FREE ebook edition is available for you or a friend with the purchase of this print book.**

CLEARLY SIGN YOUR NAME ABOVE

**Instructions to claim your free ebook edition:**
1. Visit MorganJamesBOGO.com
2. Sign your name CLEARLY in the space above
3. Complete the form and submit a photo of this entire page
4. You or your friend can download the ebook to your preferred device

ISBN 9781636984292 paperback
ISBN 9781636984308 ebook
Library of Congress Control Number:
2024932090

**Cover Design by:**
Chris Treccani
www.3dogcreative.net

**Interior Design by:**
Christopher Kirk
www.GFSstudio.com

Morgan James is a proud partner of Habitat for Humanity Peninsula and Greater Williamsburg. Partners in building since 2006.

Get involved today! Visit: www.morgan-james-publishing.com/giving-back

# DEDICATION

*For Kim, Fred, and our families who encouraged and*
*stood by us on this transformational journey.*
*Love You More!*

# TABLE OF CONTENTS

# ACKNOWLEDGMENTS

Our hope is that this book kicks off a movement of people taking responsibility for their relationships, being intentional about building trust, experiencing the positive transformation, and sharing it with others.

The journey that got us here begins with the influence our parents had on our lives. Their love and a foundation of faith and family provided an extraordinary place to start. There are so many people that influenced us throughout our lives that each played an important part in shaping how we build, cultivate, repair and restore trust in our relationships.

Roy...

- Kim, the hero of my story and the most loving and grace-filled person I've ever known and the greatest champion of this idea.
- My children, Roy, Ben, Sam, and Faith, who have listened to me talk about this their whole lives.
- My father and mother, Roy and Suzy Reid, and sisters Jenny and Kathy, who provided a strong foundation of faith, hope and love.

- Mark Hayes and the Stockworth team, who are helping me bring *The Trust Transformation* to people every day.
- Jimmie Ferrell, Director of Student Services at the University of Central Florida and founder of the O-Team, where so much of what I learned framed how I foster relationships.
- Randy Berridge, whose mentorship was all about the power of relationships.
- Grand Masters Glenn Wilson, David Turnbull, and Kathy Wieczerza for their teaching, guidance, and support in my journey as
- a martial artist.
- Wendy Kurtz, who took me to a book writing conference in 2007, where I began to outline these concepts, and her advocacy of our idea to Morgan James Publishing.
- Randy Haffner, CEO, AdventHealth Florida, who hired me as his Marketing and Public Relations Manager for Volusia Medical Center, where the seeds of most of what's in this book were planted.
- John Sowinski, Tre Evers, Michelle Edwards, Mandy Taylor, Hue Lien Duxbury, and Jessie Blakely, my colleagues at Consensus Communications, where I first launched an idea called Outrageous Trust.
- Pam Nabors, Wendy Brandon, Russ Suddeth, who were the first to bring the Outrageous Trust training to their teams, adopt the Trust Contract and provide continual feedback as to how it helped foster high trust cultures in their companies.
- My clients and people that allow me to share this life-changing information every day.

Omayra…

- Fred, my husband who has allowed me to grow as a person and encouraged me to be a leader who leads with her heart. You have loved me and encouraged me to pursue what brings me joy and I am so grateful that you are my forever partner in life.

- My kids, Liz and Alex, who have taught me more about myself and about living fulfilling moments than I ever expected! For reminding me every day that there are little joys to celebrate and for allowing me to learn and grow as a mom.

- My parents and sisters, Edwin, Lizzie, Michelle and Carmen, who have demonstrated to me, Fred, Liz, and Alex how to lead lives committed to strong relationships, caring for each other, and rooted in faith. You are such a blessing to your family, friends and communities.

- My two best friends, Brooke and Katy, who set the standard for what makes an authentic relationship, and who are the advocates I can call at three in the morning without hesitation.

- Extraordinary leaders - Tim Clark, Jo Ann Ankoviak, Eulanie Lashley, and Katie Carroll, who were early adopters, demonstrated humility and vulnerability in learning these concepts as a team and made the commitment to lead with trust. Your dedication to our community and patients continues to inspire me.

- My mentors, Mark Hertling, Lieutenant General, US Army (retired) and Neil Finkler, MD, former Chief Clinical Officer, AdventHealth, for investing in me as a physician leader and caring for me as a person. You set the standard for what trusted professionals should be.

Both of us…

- Todd Chobotar, Denise Putt, Stacy Tol, Lillian Boyd, Danica Eylenstein, Michelle Dolske PhD and the team at AdventHealth Press for taking an idea and shaping it into The Trust Transformation training program and now a book.

- Leah Gossai, Ellie Lang, Sarah Hawkins, Nate Gonzalez and the AdventHealth Health and Well Being education and training team, who brought the program to thousands of team members at AdventHealth. Through their partnership during the pandemic, we offered a safe place for team members to regularly get together virtually to talk, share, cry and support one another in the framework of trust.
- Terry Shaw, CEO of AdventHealth for his leadership and advocacy of trust throughout the organization, and especially during the pandemic.
- David Hancock and the entire team at Morgan James Publishing for bringing the book to the world.
- The thousands of AdventHealth team members who've taken The Trust Transformation course, advocated for it and demonstrated it in the care they give.

# FOREWORD

Trust. Hard to gain and easy to destroy. When trust is present, it allows for speed in decision making, failures to be forgiven, and outcomes to flourish. It moves the conversation from me to we and creates unbreakable bonds of support that can endure the toughest of times.

With 20 years of leadership experience, I have seen the fullness of the rewards that trust can have on an organization or in personal lives. I have also seen the other side where words are just words and actions are void. At the intersection of trust and mistrust is one simple word-Choice. Each of us get to choose what type of leader, spouse, son or daughter we want to be. In trusting relationships those wants turn to actions and those actions over time weave a network of memories that allow trust to abide.

*The Trust Transformation* boldly tackles the core components that can build or erode trust throughout our lives. It moves you through the importance of building lasting relationships and identifies core behaviors that foster trusting environments. It will take you on a journey that will have you explore your personal brand and how faith can play a role in personal and professional relationships. Simply put, there are many dynamics to achieve the highest levels of trust and this book takes you through each concept in an organized and reflective manner.

I have had the opportunity to personally use the content of this book to build better relationships in both my personal and professional life. Like with most things, you will only get out of it what you are willing to invest in it. Building trust and relationships is no different. It takes work, but the rewards can last a lifetime and produce unimaginable results.

–**Tim Clark**
CEO, AdventHealth Heart of Florida

# THE JOURNEY TO TRANSFORMATIONAL TRUST

A s a partner in a public relations firm that specialized in high-stakes communications during times of crises, I (Roy Reid) wanted to convey the importance of ethical behavior to my clients. I found I could do this quite effectively through the lens of trust. Most everyone can understand the need for trust in both personal and professional relationships. To teach the business leaders I worked with methods for earning, building, and restoring trust in their relationships, I developed a daylong seminar entitled *Outrageous Trust.* The course taught trust-building principles and culminated in a written commitment from participants to apply what they had learned. In the weeks and months that followed, clients consistently reported positive transformations in behavior, relationships, and culture.

Moved by the positive results of the training and convicted that trust is vital for professional as well as personal relationships, I grew more and more passionate about the topic and decided to make career moves that would allow me to increase my focus on helping people improve their performance and results through this trust program. In 2013, I began work at the University of Central Florida's College of Business, where I was able to train the staff of ten departments and many outside organizations and ventures on developing trusting relationships.

Three years later, I accepted the position for executive director of communications at AdventHealth. Almost immediately, I began to look for ways I could collaborate with the company and build a community of trust.

## The Trust Transformation

AdventHealth offers its employees various education courses for improving their health and well-being. I was asked by the publishing team to create a four-hour curriculum on trust building, based on *Outrageous Trust*, that would further examine the health and well-being benefits experienced by participants afterwards with follow-up research. To do so, I needed to recruit a co-author with a clinical background so we could delve deeper into the health benefits of trust. Dr. Omayra Mansfield—then chief of staff and physician leader in the emergency department of AdventHealth Celebration—was an easy choice, as she was passionate for these issues and an advocate for the well-being of clinicians.

Prior to becoming a physician, Dr. Mansfield worked in healthcare as a hospital administrator in a large academic setting. As an administrator, she witnessed firsthand the opportunity that existed to significantly impact patient clinical outcomes as well as business performance if there is a focus on intentionally building strong relationships with clinical stakeholders. While practicing as an attending physician, she also experienced the benefits and consequences when administrators and physicians communicated effectively or not. Additionally, Dr. Mansfield saw the impact that a lack of focus on strong relationships had on patient experience as well as the rising burnout of her clinical colleagues.

She knew that if we focused and brought these principles to the clinical teams, we would be promoting their own well-being as well as the delivery of patient care.

With our marching orders, we developed *The Trust Transformation*.

*The Trust Transformation* provided participants with tools to cultivate trust and a structure that reframed how they perceived their roles and responsibilities for building trust. That shift in understanding and acceptance of a higher degree of accountability was critical to the resulting transformations they experienced in their lives.

AdventHealth conducted a study approved by its Institutional Review Board (IRB) to identify the impact that intentional trust-building training had on subjects who had taken *The Trust Transformation* and on those around them. The study considered the influence on participants' feelings, their management of trust, their self-perception and self-confidence, and their perception of others.

## Research Findings

Biostatistician Julie Pepe helped identify the following key behavioral impacts from *The Trust Transformation* and statistically significant changes reported by participants:

- Heightened awareness and greater intentionality regarding trust in relationships
- A more optimistic outlook and positive expectations for successful outcomes
- A stronger sense of trust in themselves (trustworthiness)
- Less fear of confronting challenging situations and bringing important issues to light
- Greater self-confidence in dealing with change
- Greater self-confidence in decision-making within a moral framework

While additional research is necessary—including long-term studies of the program's influence on participants' performance at work, their health, and other aspects of their lives—it's evident that intentionality in trust building makes a profound improvement in one's relationships. Further, trust building begins from within; will positively affect one's confidence, outlook, and self-view; and fortifies the participant to make lasting, transformational changes.

Based on the positive reported outcomes, AdventHealth continues to offer *The Trust Transformation* curriculum to its employees. To date, nearly five thousand AdventHealth team members have taken the course. In addition, thousands of people outside of AdventHealth have experienced *The Trust Transformation* through workshops, speeches, podcasts, and programs we've conducted over the past few years.

We see this effort as a movement to help people improve their health and performance by improving their relationships with a more intentional focus on trust. Thank you for joining the movement by reading *The Trust Transformation* and putting these ideas to work in your life.

If you would like to learn more and find additional resources for building trust, visit our website TheTrustTransformation.com.

# A CALL TO ACTION AND TRANSFORMATION

*"Trust is the highest form of human motivation. It brings out the very best in people. But it takes time and patience, and it doesn't preclude the necessity to train and develop people so that their competency can rise to the level of that trust."*
~Stephen R. Covey

The need for trust is crucial. It is the foundation on which relationships are built. Growth, innovation, transformation, and restoration occur through relationships. Relationships are the cornerstone to success in every aspect of our lives and the channel by which we accomplish great things. Without trust, personal and professional relationships alike are hampered by resentments, suspicions, and failed communication.

In the public arena, distrust only seems to grow as we weather global health crises, racial injustice, social unrest, and unrelenting political disputes. Unfortunately, the prevalence and accessibility of unreliable sources of information hasn't helped. On any given day, stories of broken trust play out on the news, on social media, and in the private and professional lives of millions.

Research shows a significant decrease in trust in recent years. The Edelman Trust Barometer shows a loss of trust in government leaders, religious leaders, journalists, and CEOs. And trust has trended down in all sources of information, including search engines, traditional media, owned media, and social media.[1] The most disturbing aspect of the latest report is its statement that the default emotion for society is distrust.[2]

A study on behalf of the American Board of Internal Medicine Foundation found that a third of physicians surveyed do not trust their healthcare organization's leadership, and even fewer trust healthcare executives in general.[3]

## The Benefits of Trust

There are many advantages of high-trust relationships. According to a report by the University of Minnesota, benefits of strong personal relationships include longer life, better health, better stress management, and higher perception of well-being.[4]

Professional environments with high levels of trust have greater employee satisfaction and lower rates of turnover, and in the clinical setting demonstrate greater safety, superior clinical outcomes, and higher levels of teamwork. A study published in *The Journal of Applied Behavioral Science* found that investments that strengthened connections between people were more impactful than material incentives for improving workplace performance. High-trust relationships contribute to resilience and help mitigate some effects of burnout.[5]

Dr. Jo Shapiro of Harvard Medical School calls professionalism an umbrella term for "behaviours that support trustworthy relationships."[6] A culture of professional behaviors and relationships contributes to a professional community and has a beneficial impact on team member well-being and patient safety.[7] Team behaviors, technical abilities, and cognitive responses can be impacted by unprofessional relationships. Focusing on developing stronger trusting relationships can yield notable benefits in high-stake professions.

The Harvard Study of Adult Development found a significant association between happiness and meaningful relationships like those with a spouse, other family members, and close friends. This longitudinal study began tracking the health of 268 Harvard sophomores in 1938 and followed them for eighty years.[8] The goal was to discover clues to healthy and happy lives.

"Personal connection creates mental and emotional stimulation, which are automatic mood boosters, while isolation is a mood buster," says project director Dr. Robert Waldinger. "This is also an opportunity to focus on positive relationships and let go of negative people in your life, or at least minimize your interactions with them."[9]

## The Time Is Now

Trust is a living element within our relationships with the capacity to grow or diminish depending on the effort we put into it. If you are satisfied with average levels of trust, then you concede the best life has to offer. If, however, you learn to be intentional about earning, cultivating, and repairing trust, your outlook and life experiences will be transformed.

Our passion is to teach people—to teach *you*—the critical steps needed to build stronger relationships with others and with yourself. We will show you how to become mindful of trust, to take responsibility for your relationships, and to adjust your perspective. We will help you to consider the current state of trust in your life and take crucial action to improve it. At the end of each chapter, you will find an activity or set of reflection questions designed to review the material covered and help you to personally apply it.

Because our physical, mental, and emotional well-being are integrally linked, taking care of ourselves is a critical component of building trust.

In chapter ten, we discuss seven specific behaviors critical to maintaining health and balance in life.

We are already confident of the significant impact trust building can have on you—we've seen its positive effects in the lives of so many others. The question is, are you ready to do the work to achieve strong, lasting relationships and experience transformational changes in your own life? This is your personal invitation to join a movement to elevate trust and transform society . . . one person at a time.

-Roy Reid, APR, CPRC, & Omayra Mansfield, MD

*CHAPTER ONE*

# WHEN YOUR WORLD IS MOVED

*"Sometimes, when things fall apart, well,*
*that's the big opportunity to change."*
~Pema Chodron

I t was early evening on Good Friday, March 27, 1964. Families in Anchorage, Alaska, were preparing for dinner or out and about, enjoying the holiday evening, when suddenly and violently, the ground began to reel. Just off the coast in Prince William Sound, a buildup of friction between the earth's continental and oceanic crusts gave way, leading to a megathrust earthquake and a fault rupture six hundred miles long. For four and a half minutes, the streets rolled like ocean waves. Buildings toppled, sidewalks ripped from the roads, and utility pipes burst as the earth spasmed.

The magnitude 9.2 earthquake was the second most powerful in recorded history. It could be felt throughout Alaska and as far away as Seattle (1,200 miles) where it swayed the Space Needle.[10] Nine people died as a direct result of the quake, but 122 more perished from the landslides and tsunamis that followed and wreaked havoc on nearly every Alaskan coastal town as well as most of the other Pacific beaches in the US—all the way to Hawaii. In addition to the property and infrastructure damage as well as the tragic loss of life, the unforeseen natural disaster permanently changed the landscape—raising some areas of land by thirty feet, lowering others by eight feet, and redrawing many coastlines.[11] Reflect on that for a moment . . . It's hard to comprehend how such a short span of time could lead to such catastrophic changes. How one moment life was stable, and the next, life changed forever.

So, what does the 1964 earthquake have to do with trust? We think it's a good metaphor for the reality-changing issues each of us may face in life—the death or birth of a loved one, marriage or divorce, a new job or a job loss. We also may expect an onslaught of accompanying issues with these types of major life shifts. We can't stop change from happening, but we can control how we prepare for and react to it.

Following the Alaska quake, we achieved a better understanding of the causes of earthquakes and the function of plate tectonics. Determined to be more prepared in the future, experts committed to finding ways to use science to minimize the negative impact of quakes. The United States Geological Survey (USGS) Earthquake Hazards Program was established, as well as the National Oceanic and Atmospheric Administration's (NOAA's) 24/7 tsunami warning system. New building codes were mandated, and older buildings were retrofitted to meet new standards. All of these developments work in concert now to provide better outcomes when disaster strikes.

It is through our relationships that we can prepare for, recover from, and even thrive in the midst of many of life's most challenging issues. One of our fundamental beliefs is that we are created for connection and that in good times and bad, we see positive changes in our lives when we improve our relationships. The foundation of this book is that trust is the key factor in cultivating the most fulfilling and productive relationships.

When we have high-trust relationships, with ourselves and with others, it fortifies our resilience and supports effective recovery from broken trust. Trust is also a catalyst for greater health and well-being and provides us the benefit of the doubt when we make a mistake or confront a crisis.

It's not the issue or crisis that defines us, but how we respond to and deal with it that frames us going forward. Trust is the bedrock for our relationships. It guides us through the most seismic issues we face as well as much smaller aspects of our daily lives.

## What Is Transformational Trust and How Does It Work?

If we're going to help trust flourish in our lives, we need to study its components. Trust is not an inert object, but a complex, living entity that can grow or weaken by our actions and the impact of external forces.

**Trust (n)**—*Assured reliance on the character, ability, strength, or truth of someone or something*[12]

There are some extraordinary expectations associated with trust. In order for a person to be perceived as trustworthy, others evaluate their character, ability, strength, and honesty.

After many years of studying trust both personally and professionally, we've developed the following list of some fundamental truths about trust:

- Trust must be earned.
- Trust is the foundation for reputation and brand.
- Trust contributes to perceptions of competency and integrity.
- Trust is the license to grow and change and the currency for moving things forward.
- Trust is the "benefit of the doubt" when times are difficult.
- Trust is your anchor.
- Trust is often overlooked and assumed—despite its importance.
- Trust is your responsibility.

Trust, like a gift, is given—to us or by us—so it is a choice that can be made by the minute and in the moment. Therefore, it is essential to be *intentional* in our efforts to build trusting relationships.

## Little Things Can Transform Us

Sometimes we learn more about something when we fail. This is one of those stories. It began on the Friday of Memorial Day weekend several years ago.

First, you need to understand that I (Roy) and my daughter, Faith, have a close and strong connection. She is the youngest of four children and the only girl. As I arrived home from work, Faith, who was seven at the time, rushed to meet me at the door and nearly knocked me over with her breathless excitement.

"Daddy, I made something for you. Come see, come see!"

Pulling my hand, she led us through the house and into the dining room where I saw what appeared to be a bead factory explosion. The entire dining room table (and much of the floor) was covered with colorful plastic beads, rubber bands, and other tools necessary to produce plastic jewelry.

"Look what I made for you, Daddy," said Faith, holding up a beautiful bead bracelet. "Will you wear it?"

"Absolutely, I'll wear it!" I said, and immediately put it on. "Tell me about it."

Faith excitedly explained how she had spent a good portion of the day carefully and skillfully making the colorful bracelet especially for me. Her eyes sparkled and she beamed with joy as I admired her handiwork and thanked her profusely for such an exquisite accessory to my wardrobe.

I wore that bracelet everywhere we went during the entire long holiday weekend. And Faith took great pride in showing it off to people. If you are a parent and have ever received a gift to wear, you know that you instantly become your child's "show and tell" for everyone you meet.

Dressing for work on Tuesday morning, I realized I would need to wear a suit because I had some critical client meetings that day. Without a second thought, I took off the bracelet, laid it on my dresser, and headed to work.

As I arrived home that evening, I noticed that Faith still had the bracelet factory going full force in our dining room. Sometime later while I was helping my wife, Kim, with dinner, Faith came up to me in the kitchen with a newly made bracelet with different colored beads. My first thought was, "Oh dear . . . I only have so much arm to give to the cause." But her next sentence would forever change my perspective.

With a hurt yet hopeful look on her face, Faith said, "Daddy, if you don't like the other bracelet, will you wear this one?"

Looking down at my barren wrist, I realized at that moment that Faith believed I had removed her handmade gift because I didn't like it.

If you are a parent, you know the feeling of despair when you see that your child is hurt, and for a moment, I could not even talk as my inner voice screamed at me for breaking my daughter's trust.

Of course, I rationalized that Faith didn't understand I couldn't wear a plastic bead bracelet to work in my suit. But then, I remembered that the following month I was to teach a room full of people in my profession how they should be more intentional in matters of trust. I had twenty-plus years of experience in communications and aspired to be a thought leader on trust; nevertheless, I stood there speechless and crushed.

That moment was my most humbling, and I will forever be grateful for it. Because in that moment, I was transformed by trust.

Faith heard me say, "Absolutely, I will wear it." I had made a commitment to her with no caveats or qualifiers. Then, I hadn't kept my word.

WOW! I had broken trust with my daughter because I didn't think through all the implications of my commitment. I was not trying to pull a fast one on Faith. I did not set out to hurt her. I was not conspiring to take anything away from her. She is my daughter, and I would never purposefully harm her. I simply was not intentional about trying to understand Faith's perspective and expectations.

Standing there in my kitchen, I gained exceptional clarity of what people must know about trust, and what I needed to do. Though I was about to train my first national audience on trust, I had just blown it with a seven-year-old over a plastic bead bracelet. Some expert!

So, what did I do next? I apologized to her for not keeping my word, dropped everything I was doing, and immediately put the bracelet back on.

I wear the bracelet every day now and have for years. It has not come off, except for some minor repair work. I wear it for two reasons. First, because I told my daughter I would. Second, and most importantly to this lesson, because it reminds me that every little thing I say or do either contributes to or diminishes the trust others have placed in me.

## Humility: The Key That Unlocks Transformational Trust

This teachable moment with Faith crystalizes a vital concept that is foundational to all that follows. In order to build and protect trust with others, you must be humble or willing to become humble. We all make mistakes. At various times and in numerous ways, each of us will let others down. We will fail to keep our promises, we will intentionally or unintentionally hurt others, and we will make decisions that don't work out well for everyone involved. As a result, we need to have the willingness to correct our actions, ask for forgiveness, or make amends. These steps require humility. We must be humble and take a proactive and intentional approach to building trust if we're going to cultivate, earn, maintain, and transform our relationships.

Humility is also essential for us to develop empathy, which is necessary for gaining a deeper understanding and appreciation for the beliefs, emotions, and experiences of others. Empathy fosters a strong sense of understanding and an emotional connection in our relationships.

We will come back to the concept of humility over and over again throughout this book to demonstrate all the ways it is useful in building trust. But for now, we must understand that humility is the key that unlocks transformational trust in our relationships.

When the incident with Roy's daughter occurred, he could easily have blown it off. However, he consciously decided to try to see the situation from her side and understand how his actions affected her. He knew that we build trust or tear it down one step, one action, and one person at a time.

Now, some may say, "It's just a plastic bead bracelet we're talking about." True, yet that perspective illustrates a problem we face every day. We tend to overlook the feelings and expectations of others, thinking them unimportant; however, those small things will eventually add up to become big problems if left unaddressed. Even small broken promises can potentially lead to a major breach of trust that could have been avoided.

Being considered trustworthy is about the perceptions and beliefs others have of us. It's the little things that matter when building trust. Small deposits of trust build interest and eventually become great vaults of trust, especially when they are made consistently over time.

At one point or another, we have been in each of the two positions the bracelet story illustrates. We've been the parent who in the busy, fast-paced schedule of the day breaks a commitment, carelessly says something, or even worse, doesn't deliver something promised. And we have been the child who loses faith in someone who has broken their word, failed to deliver, said something insulting, or treated us badly.

We all know how broken trust feels, and we will at times break trust with someone else, even unintentionally, and must deal with the fallout.

**If we understand that trust is earned and if we take respon-sibility for our relationships, those relationships will become more fulfilling, productive, and enriching.** As the gospel of Luke says:

> *Whoever can be trusted with very little can also be trusted with much, and whoever is dishonest with very little will also be dishonest with much.*[13]

Taking responsibility for our relationships requires humility. In his worldwide best-selling book *The Purpose Driven Life*, Rick Warren said, "Humility is not thinking less of yourself; it's thinking of yourself less."[14] Approaching relationships with a humble attitude is the first step to unlocking the other person's trust in us.

*TIME* magazine published an article entitled "Humility, a Quiet, Unappreciated Strength," which opens with the line, "Humility doesn't top the list of popular virtues these days, but if you're ever in need of help, a humble friend is more likely to be there for you than a prideful one," citing research published in the *Journal of Positive Psychology*.[15] When we exercise greater humility in our lives, we are more likely to step into a role of being more intentional and mindful of others—a quality that leads to greater trust.

Many of us aren't naturally humble; in fact, some of us may identify with the old song that says it's hard to be humble when we're already perfect! But being humble can be learned and cultivated if you're willing to put in the time and effort.

Being humble doesn't mean you're insecure, a pushover, or a door-mat. On the contrary, humility means you recognize your limitations and your strengths and weaknesses, and you keep your talents and accomplishments in correct perspective. Humble people focus on the welfare of others rather than themselves. They have a genuine interest in others and treat them with respect. Humble people know their self-worth and don't need to toot their own horn.

To develop humility, you must . . .

- **Be other-focused**. As Rick Warren expresses it, think of yourself less; it's not all about you.
- **Act on your concern for others**. Lend a hand when you see a need.
- **Treat everyone equally**. As fellow human beings, everyone with whom you come in contact is worthy of respect and dignity.
- **Accept critical feedback**. We all have areas in which we can grow and learn.
- **Cultivate gratitude**. Look for opportunities to be thankful for something or someone.
- **Admit your wrongs**. If you make a mistake, admit it, and fix it to the best of your ability.
- **Listen first**. Speak less. Develop great listening skills. Engage fully with others by giving them your undivided attention.

## The Trust Boost

Since trust is a choice, you can choose to take certain actions to make it easier for others to trust you. We call these actions trust boosts. Throughout this book, we're going to be sharing with you many strategies you can implement to build trust, but here's a trust boost teaser:

Be dependable.

Be a person of your word, and take your word seriously. When you say you're going to meet your friend at a specific time, make sure you are there on time or early. When you promise to do something for a colleague, don't let it slip your mind and fall through the cracks. Others you live and work with will come to know that they can trust you to do what you say you'll do.

## The Trust Bust

In the same way specific positive actions and behaviors can build people's ability to trust us, negative behaviors will cause them to distrust us. We refer to these as trust busting. We'll be sharing behaviors to avoid in order not to bust trust.

Take, for instance, the opposite of the trust booster mentioned above: being undependable. It's easy to see how, if we're always late or don't follow through with our promises, people will have a hard time trusting us. Trust-busting behaviors are ones you'll want to shun as you seek to build sustainable trust relationships.

## Reflection

1.  Recall a time when you broke someone's trust. How did it feel? Were you able to repair it? If so, how?
2.  Think of three people you trust most in your life. What words would you use to describe them? (You will refer to this list in chapter four.)
3.  Which of the seven ways for developing humility listed above could you work on?

# CHAPTER TWO

# WE ARE BUILT FOR RELATIONSHIPS

*"Success in any relationship or endeavor begins with trust."*
~S. Truett Cathy

When Paul Jarley, PhD, was appointed dean of the University of Central Florida (UCF) College of Business in 2012, he immediately set out to transform the culture at the college, which had grown very transactional over the preceding decade. UCF had expanded exponentially in that same period. With more than seventy thousand full-time students, UCF had become the biggest university in the United States.

The college of business was one of the largest within the university with nearly ten thousand students. To accommodate the growth, many of the classes were sizeable and able to be facilitated through a lecture-capture format—significantly limiting the personal engagement between faculty members and students.

"I believe true learning occurs when two people sit down together and have a conversation about something interesting," said Jarley about the kind of culture he hoped to inspire. "Students need more engagement with our faculty in addition to business leaders and alumni that can help them become successful."

Personal engagement would require people to take responsibility for their relationships more intentionally. Jarley knew this would take a significant effort to realize, and it had to begin with him. One of the first things he did following his appointment set the stage for the changes he wished to put in motion.

The college of business has more than two hundred faculty and staff. To ensure that Jarley had an opportunity to hear from every team member, he scheduled a one-on-one meeting with each person in his office. His agenda was simple: hear everyone's ideas for working to create a culture built on engagement and relationships.

"Those meetings were important in helping me fully understand the culture and how we could make the changes necessary to transform it," Jarley says. "The most frequent comment I got from our team was, 'So, this is what the dean's office looks like,' because most had never been in there before."

The meetings set a new tone and the expectation that the college and its leaders were going to be engaged. Programs and events would be established to encourage involvement and conversations. A student ambassador initiative was created to prompt student participation, advocate involvement and opportunities to the student body, and reach out to partners to increase interactions with the college. In addition, Jarley reorganized the academic advisory office into the Office of Professional Development and staffed it with human resources professionals to ensure the student experience led students toward a professional career.

The college quickly reflected the desired culture, and a number of new programs sprung up to support it. Within two years, the college of business garnered national attention for the changes and in 2016 was recognized by *US News & World Report's* ranking of best colleges for the first time in its history.[16]

In 2020, I (Omayra) was appointed Chief Medical Officer (CMO) at AdventHealth Apopka. The hospital had recently been relocated into a brand-new facility, providing the opportunity to create a fresh impression in the community. Recognizing the potential of the moment, I approached my transition to this new role in a way similar to Dean Jarley's. I scheduled one-on-one meetings with each member of the team to get their insights on the clinical situation and opportunities for improvement.

This investment in relationships, in conjunction with *The Trust Transformation* program taken by the leadership of AdventHealth Apopka (discussed in chapter three), became foundational as the clinical team confronted the COVID-19 pandemic of 2020–2022.

Our community hospital was licensed for 119 beds, but inpatient volume soared to 150 at the peak of the delta variant surge. We had to put patients in different spaces—including our preoperative area—and hold patients in our emergency department. We had a nineteen-bed intensive care unit with twenty-three patients and another four ICU patients waiting for a place in the emergency department. At one point, one-fifth of all our patients were on mechanical ventilators, and another fifth were on heated high-flow oxygen—often a precursor to intubation. We stopped surgeries to allow for the redeployment of nursing staff to support these overflow spaces. Despite all these efforts, we felt we couldn't keep up with critically ill patients needing to be seen in our emergency department. We actually had to bring oxygen to patients who were still in the waiting room.

The early investment of time with each member of the clinical team produced strong, well-developed relationships and established the expectation that those relationships would be prioritized. At the height of the pandemic, when our facilities and services were completely overwhelmed, we experienced the dividends of those investments as our teams pulled together, supported each other, solved problems, and provided the care our community needed.

When leaders recognize that we are created for relationships, lead with trust, fortify relationships, and set high expectations for personal interactions, the difference within an organization is palpable. Investments in people change the dynamic.

## Relationships Are Essential

Relationships are essential in our lives. All of us are created with an inherent desire to have strong interpersonal connections that contribute to our life and well-being. We humans are wired for relationships with others. We must strive to build those relationships on a foundation that ensures they are nurtured in good times and bad.

A significant number of research studies have shown that positive, healthy relationships are a vital part of well-being and performance, and that people with these kinds of associations have a much higher quality of life and improved outcomes in the workplace.[17] Conversely, those without a strong social structure suffer more adverse health conditions, struggles in their careers, and limited opportunities.

An article from the University of Minnesota demonstrates some of the significant positive personal outcomes associated with strong relationships, including our ability to live longer, healthier lives. The piece, entitled *Why Relationships Are Important*, says that a review of 148 studies found people with strong social relationships are 50 percent less likely to die prematurely.[18] Additionally, the research from Dan Buettner's book *Blue Zones* calculates that committing to a life partner can add three years to life expectancy.[19]

Research by psychologist Sheldon Cohen identified that college students who reported having strong relationships were half as likely to catch a common cold when exposed to the virus.[20] An

AARP study with older adults found that loneliness is a significant predictor of poor health.[21] More generally, an international Gallup poll found that people who feel they have friends and family to count on are more satisfied with their personal health than people who feel isolated.[22]

Strong relationships can impact your perception of your own well-being as well as your ability to recover from stress. A survey of five thousand people by the National Bureau of Economic Research found that doubling your group of friends has the same effect on your well-being as a 50 percent increase in income. In a separate study of over one hundred people, researchers found that people who completed a stressful task experienced a faster recovery when they were reminded of people with whom they had strong, positive relationships. On the other hand, those who were reminded of stressful relationships experienced even more stress and higher blood pressure.[23]

Conversely, when we don't invest in building strong relationships, we suffer negative consequences. Studies demonstrate these consequences include increased rates of depression, decreased immune function, and negative pathophysiological changes. For example, researchers at the University of Chicago found in a five-year study that loneliness could predict higher blood pressure even years down the road.[24]

Strong relationships dramatically improve our professional lives as well, and this positive impact is front and center in the workplace. A research study published in the *Journal of Applied Behavioral Science* demonstrates that investments aimed at strengthening the connection between people are a better catalyst (as opposed to material incentives) for improved performance. Kim Cameron and his colleagues found that reinforcing certain behaviors in a workplace provided greater outcomes and benefits than deploying new processes. These behaviors include:

- Caring for, being interested in, and maintaining responsibility for colleagues as friends
- Providing support for one another, including offering kindness and compassion when others are struggling
- Avoiding the "blame game" and forgiving mistakes
- Inspiring one another
- Emphasizing the meaning of the work
- Treating one another with respect, gratitude, trust, and integrity[25]

## Improved Relationships = Improved Results

We find that relationships with a foundation of trust are stronger, produce personal benefits, and lead to better professional results.

A research study entitled "Exploring the Influence of Trust Relationships on Motivation in the Health Sector: A Systematic Review"[26] compiled articles reporting research findings from a ten-year period and reviewed the results as it related to healthcare workers' motivation and performance, and the impact of trusted relationships on their outcomes. The study's conclusion cites a number of encouraging ideas related to the impact of relationships and results. "Evidence indicates that workplace trust relationships encourage social interactions and cooperation among healthcare workers, have impact on the intrinsic motivation of healthcare workers and have consequences for retention, performance, and quality of care. Human resource management and organizational practices are critical in sustaining workplace trust and healthcare workers' motivation. Research and assessment of the levels of motivation and factors that encourage workplace trust relationships should include how trust and motivation interact and operate for retention, performance, and quality of care."

The impact that trust can have when reinforced and tended to can often be understated. Relationships fortified by trust can change the course of a crisis. Crises come in many forms. Consider the importance of addressing trust when a crisis involves family issues or customer experiences gone wrong. We believe trust is needed to create a sustainable organization or reinvigorate a church congregation. Trust can also move a country into greater long-term prosperity.

## Four Kinds of Relationships in Our Lives

Now that we understand how important good interpersonal relationships are, let's look at four categories we have developed to demonstrate the kinds of relationships we have in our lives. Each has specific attributes and unique ways in which they may affect us. The amount of work required for each type of relationship will vary depending on the circumstance. Let's unpack the four types of relationships in our lives to better understand the way trust manifests in each one. *(Figure 2.1)*

**Advocates** are the people in your life who will always be there to fight for you.

They are the family members and closest friends who have your back no matter what.

**Allies** are people who are likely to agree with and support you but need a little encouragement to engage. These are often friends and colleagues with whom you regularly interact.

The third category, **agnostics**, is the largest. These are people who don't have an opinion of you or have not yet entered your sphere of influence. They are often misidentified as adversaries due to their lack of engagement. But don't confuse a lack of engagement with a lack of concern. If you do, you may miss out on some important opportunities.

Finally, the fourth group of people is **adversaries**. This group is comprised of people you don't trust or, conversely, who don't trust you. It may be that they are not yet willing to share their trust with you. They may have a preconceived idea of why you are not to be trusted or a general assumption of you based on external influences. You may have done something—intentionally or unintentionally—to earn their distrust (yes, we can earn distrust as well).

## Graph of Four Relationships

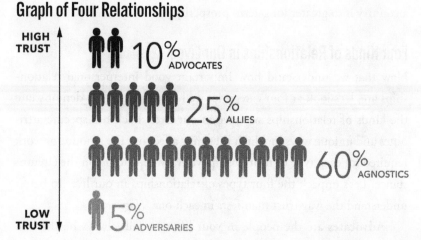

*Figure 2.1*

It is important to understand that you will always have each of these kinds of people in your life. These categories are not meant to define these relationships as "good" or "bad" but to provide you with a tool to help you better understand how trust is working and where you can take actions to improve it.

Through humility and an intentional effort to cultivate trust, and by better understanding the status of the relationship, you can adopt a mindset that keeps you from classifying these kinds of relationships as simply "good" or "bad," and probe deeper to better understand the person and their motives. In so doing, you can move people into a more fulfilling, productive, and enriching place in your life. This idea is the fuel for the engine of fostering transformational trust.

## How Do These Types of People Show Up in Your Life?

Think about people in your life, whether family, friends, or work colleagues. Who would you identify as an advocate, ally, agnostic, or adversary? How does the relationship feel and how do you deal with it? As we go forward, think about these people and how trust—or lack of it—is impacting your relationship with them.

Sometimes understanding why some of the people on our list are in the category they're in can be difficult. Part of our work is to put the relationships into perspective to better appreciate what is within our "locus of control"—or sphere of influence to make a difference—or to let go.

You will not always earn the highest level of trust. However, when you commit to the effort, you will put yourself in a position that has a positive impact on everyone in your sphere of influence. Likely you will have a significant number of people in the two middle categories of allies and agnostics, and small groups of people in the more extreme categories, advocates and adversaries.

## Trust and Relationships Are Intertwined

Notice how people work together, and it is not hard to find that the level at which they trust each other contributes to the output and the outcomes of their work.

The world around us is changing, bringing a greater intensity regarding relationships; people are more skeptical and demanding of more transparency and authenticity. Leaders—in families, businesses, and communities—must take a measure of trust, better understand it, take actions to cultivate it, and encourage people around them to be more intentional and proactive in building trust.

Trust is often misunderstood and overlooked. But you can make lasting changes by taking immediate small steps in building trust in your relationships.

**Achieving transformational trust requires an intentional focus on DOING the things that will allow you to BE trusted.**

## Activity: Time to Take Action

- Write a list of the people in your life with whom you need to build trust.
- Plan to reach out to them. Decide specifically how and when you will do so. (Make sure it is at a time and place that will make them comfortable.)
- Listen and learn what is most important to them. What are the qualities of a great listener?
- Learn what they may need. Are you able to help them?
- Find opportunities to keep engaged. How can you follow up with them?

# CHAPTER THREE

# THE OUTCOMES OF TRANSFORMATIONAL TRUST

*"There is a universal respect and even admiration
for those who are humble and simple by nature, and
who have absolute confidence in all human beings
irrespective of their social status."*
~Nelson Mandela

There is a large body of evidence supporting the importance of building relationships on a foundation of trust, demonstrating the positive outcomes associated with this work. These benefits as we have described are observed in both the personal and professional space. Understanding that this journey of transformation can be more powerful when done with others, one particular leadership group embarked on it together.

The team of executives—many new to leadership—working at AdventHealth Apopka, a recently opened facility, felt it would be wise to build strong trust relationships within the group and intentionally develop a just and transparent culture. This would foster a healthy dynamic at the top of the organization and benefit the frontline employees as well.

The executives decided to embark on *The Trust Transformation*. They each took the four-hour course on trust and were later interviewed to share what changes they observed.

Many of the leaders said that having a space where they felt safe to be vulnerable impacted how they communicated with each other. They felt free to be authentic, and they experienced the importance of presence. Many were able to better understand others by identifying their purpose. Several said that they saw positive outcomes in their personal lives as well—having more meaningful interactions with their loved ones.

The Apopka leaders subsequently faced the COVID pandemic together and observed the benefits of taking time to prioritize trust in their relationships.

Despite the many challenges the pandemic brought them and their team, their hospital saw some of the highest rates of employee and physician engagement in their large healthcare system, and significant resilience when measured objectively. In fact, the scores in these areas actually improved for their hospital during this time—something not seen elsewhere in the system.

While a number of factors contributed to these positive outcomes, at the root was a culture built on trust, a focus on authentic, transparent leadership, and leaders who were encouraged to demonstrate humility and vulnerability.

## Five Conditions of Transformational Trust

Trust fuels fulfillment, richness, and advancement in both our personal and professional relationships. In figure 3.1 you will see lists of conditions associated with trust and with distrust. Each has a personal, cultural, and (in the workplace) financial impact. High-trust conditions include having strong character, demonstrating consistency, being loyal, giving others the benefit of the doubt, and feeling confident in expected actions and behaviors. When these exist, we experience peace of mind and assurance that someone will come through. We are able to advocate for others, feel hope, and maintain a sense of safety. In the workplace, these same conditions, when present, result in reduced risk, more efficient processes, greater retention, and an ability to recover an expected brand experience.

## Trust/Distrust Outcomes

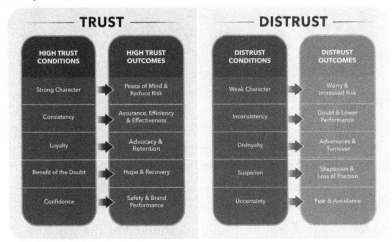

*Figure 3.1*

These critical factors listed in figure 3.1 illustrate how the presence or absence of trust in relationships has a direct impact on results. As we review these factors in more detail, consider how they already occur in your own life.

Let's take another look at the same information provided in the graphic and rearrange it a bit to demonstrate the personal and professional benefits of trust versus the negative consequences of distrust. *(Figure 3.2)*

## How Trust Transforms: The Personal and Professional Benefits of Trust

How would high-trust conditions help you, your family, and your organization? Let's review these outcomes and benefits to see what value they may offer, beginning with the foundational condition, character.

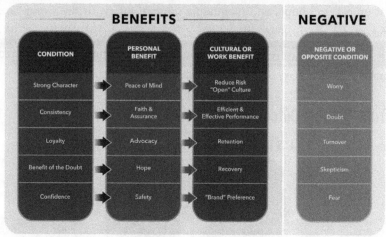

| | BENEFITS | | NEGATIVE |
|---|---|---|---|
| CONDITION | PERSONAL BENEFIT | CULTURAL OR WORK BENEFIT | NEGATIVE OR OPPOSITE CONDITION |
| Strong Character | Peace of Mind | Reduce Risk "Open" Culture | Worry |
| Consistency | Faith & Assurance | Efficient & Effective Performance | Doubt |
| Loyalty | Advocacy | Retention | Turnover |
| Benefit of the Doubt | Hope | Recovery | Skepticism |
| Confidence | Safety | "Brand" Preference | Fear |

*Figure 3.2*

A **strong**, **ethical character** gives peace of mind to the one who possesses it as well as to those around them. We feel safe being vulnerable with those we trust to do the right thing. That openness and communication help us better manage issues. If we have an ethical character, others will feel comfortable sharing with and trusting us. Two-way trust can provide a sense of calm even when crisis strikes.

Demonstrating these conditions consistently is essential to maximizing the potential for strong trust. Your **consistency** of words, behaviors, and actions offers people assurance and comfort in their relationship with you. They have faith that they will not be disturbed, disappointed, or surprised by your behavior. This tremendously impacts the positive perception people have of you. Being inconsistent, on the other hand, will cause others to doubt your trustworthiness. This uncertainty may make it difficult for them to have your back when questions arise.

Trust builds **loyalty** in our relationships, which manifests into advocacy—of you, your ideas, and your organization. People that are loyal will stick by you in good times or bad. This is true of friends, coworkers, employees, and customers. In a work setting, if people are loyal to you, they are less likely to be dissatisfied and begin looking for a different place to work. If others don't feel they can be loyal, you probably won't retain them as friends or employees. Neither will they give you the benefit of the doubt if they perceive you have broken their trust.

Knowing that others will give you the **benefit of the doubt** gives a sense of hope. When you mess up, misspeak, or break trust with people in any way (and you will), recovery is critical. The benefit of the doubt is the most important element to your recovery. When you have it, recovery begins immediately because people are more willing to accept your apology and begin rebuilding the relationship. Otherwise, you have to earn trust from scratch. If people are skeptical of you, they will not likely extend the benefit of the doubt to you.

Having a sense of safety with another person is best defined by the last condition, **confidence**. If I am confident in you, I feel safe—to be honest, do my job, or even take risks. My fears are minimized by that confidence, and there are wonderful benefits to that state of being. If people don't have confidence in you, they may be afraid to trust you or to develop a relationship with you.

Understanding the five conditions of transformational trust gives you the opportunity to ask the right questions and work to build a culture of trust around you. Make trust a part of the ongoing conversation, and provide the four guiding principles outlined in the following chapters to set expectations and accountabilities for the right behaviors. When you invest in developing greater trust in all your relationships, the outcome will always exceed your expectations.

An additional outcome worth noting is the positive health benefits of strong trust in our lives. Individuals who experience these characteristics also benefit from better health, a longer life, and a greater sense of personal well-being. They are also likely to recover more readily when they do become ill. We will spend more time on this topic in chapter ten.

Ahead, we will share principles for building trust and small steps to help you improve relationships, no matter what condition they're in at the present time. As you dive into this material, take a few minutes every day to apply the principles in ways that complement your life and lifestyle.

## Remember, It's the Little Things

Real, meaningful trust is the culmination of all the little things we say and do. We often get so caught up in the big issues surrounding trust that we forget small stuff can affect trust, improve it, and make a difference in the relationships around us.

In *The 7 Habits of Highly Effective People*, Stephen Covey refers to a similar idea with his illustration called "the emotional bank account." Every interaction we have with others either makes a deposit or a withdrawal in their emotional bank account.[27] Like our real financial accounts, if we have more deposits than withdrawals, we will find ourselves in a good position to achieve the results we desire. This means we must be mindful and intentional with our words and actions.

We have to take personal responsibility for our relationships and for cultivating trust. We must demand a high accountability of ourselves and encourage others to as well.

Relationship building takes time and intentionality, but the value of those relationships and the trust-based actions they inspire is incalculable and sometimes lifesaving. The following story is one of many we will tell to demonstrate the positive outcomes of transformational trust.

## Transformational Trust in Action

As a leader in a hospital setting, I (Omayra) round regularly on all areas of the hospital and connect with team members of all specialties and job responsibilities. Being present and getting to know individuals as people and not solely as employees is an invaluable tool in developing teams and cultivating trust. It is a constant work in progress, and the fruit of that work and effort may sometimes be surprising. This is something that I personally observed when an opportunity to leverage a strong authentic relationship arose.

During the COVID pandemic of 2020–2022, a lot of fear and uncertainty was prevalent everywhere in society, and none more so than within the walls of the hospital. As wave after wave came, questions around the illness itself, appropriate use of personal protective equipment, medical management, and other topics came and went. As leaders we had to maintain a focus on transparent relationships built on trust to be able to successfully navigate our teams during crisis. A particular team where this focus resulted in a great outcome involved our progressive care nursing unit.

In the hospital setting during COVID, our progressive care unit team was significantly impacted, as they were quickly expected to care for an increasingly complex patient population that historically was managed in the intensive care unit. This nursing team had to nimbly adapt, as patients on multiple medication drips, high-flow oxygen, and multiple co-morbidities were now within their care. On a day-to-day basis, these teams are led by assistant nurse managers who help the frontline team work through opportunities and barriers as they arise. Jennifer was a particular seasoned assistant nurse manager who was identified as a key leader and carried significant influence on the unit. When rounding on the team, I would come to get to know Jennifer, her heart for her team, and her love of her family.

As the pandemic persisted, the availability of vaccines and opportunity to receive the vaccination arose for our teams. Initially, Jennifer and the majority of the nurses on the progressive care unit refused the vaccination. They were skeptical and felt that there was not enough information available on the safety profile or efficacy of the vaccine. Interestingly, some also felt a sense of normalcy dealing with COVID, as they had managed patients with this illness for almost a year and the majority of them had not become severely ill with or contracted the disease. One by one they declined the vaccination, and even joked it would never be something they would even consider. Despite this, during my routine rounds on the units throughout the hospital, I would continue to encourage them to consider vaccination, answering questions whenever they arose and providing the most up-to-date information regarding the efficacy and safety of the vaccine.

For a brief period of time, the number of patients declined within the hospital setting, and collectively the team felt it could start to breathe. This was short lived. Within a matter of months, another surge emerged, this one the worst one yet. Once again, the progressive care unit was caring for highly complex patients. This wave, however, brought even more critically ill patients, most of them young, and almost all of them unvaccinated.

I continued to round throughout the hospital. One particular day, as per my usual routine, I stopped to chat with Jennifer to check in with her and see how I could help her team. I shared with her the most current information on the vaccine. To my surprise, she told me that she was considering getting it later in the week. I asked her what had changed her mind. She said she'd noticed that the patients in our care were younger and unvaccinated and that she wanted to make sure she did everything possible to stay healthy for the sake of her family, especially her grandson who brought her so much joy. Not wanting to miss the opportunity to have her be vaccinated, I asked her if she would be willing to receive the vaccination that same day if I could make the arrangements for her. She replied, "Yes." Much to her surprise as well as mine, I started to cry. She asked me what made me cry, and I said that it was the immense relief I had, knowing that she would be as safe as possible not only for herself but also for her family that I know she cared so deeply for.

I immediately got to work and started making the necessary calls and arrangements to allow for her to be vaccinated. The process took me an hour, and I was able to then return with a team to provide Jennifer the vaccine. Arriving back on the unit, I quickly learned that Jennifer had shared her plan with the other nurses on the same floor and explained her rationale. The trust relationship Jennifer had developed with her coworkers garnered her a significant degree of influence. Thankfully, we had brought many doses, because one by one, nurses, techs, and paramedics lined up to be vaccinated. Word quickly spread throughout the hospital, and by the end of that day, Jennifer and sixty-one other employees who had previously declined the vaccination received it.

As I was preparing to leave for the day, I walked back upstairs to the progressive care unit. I found Jennifer. I looked at her and said, "Sixty-one." She asked me what that meant. I told her that because of her, sixty-one of her colleagues were one step closer to being safer from this terrible illness. Because of the trust relationships she had built, her level of influence that came from being trusted, and the courage she demonstrated, our work family was safer.

## Reflection

1. Have you ever spent a long time in a personal or professional environment with high-trust conditions? How about one with low-trust conditions? What significant differences did you notice in their operations or outcomes?

2. Do you balance the emotional interactions you have with others, or do you find yourself making more withdrawals than deposits?

3. Do you recall a time when an individual was able to achieve a tremendous outcome by appropriately leveraging their influence and trustworthiness?

# CHAPTER FOUR

# THE ATTRIBUTES AND GUIDING PRINCIPLES OF TRANSFORMATIONAL TRUST

*"Few things can help an individual more
than to place responsibility on him, and
to let him know that you trust him."*
~Booker T. Washington

Recognizing that relationships require work is only part of the equation in creating stronger trust-filled connections. A critical element is owning your part of the relationship and your responsibility for the work. This takes courage and humility (there's that word again). I (Omayra) discovered this shortly after I first learned the attributes of trust.

As Roy and I discussed how we achieve transformational trust and the corresponding principles, I thought I understood. The ideas resonated with me. It's trust, right? How hard can it be? It's a word we use frequently and probably don't think too much about.

A few weeks after hearing of these concepts and attributes, I had my first of what would be many "aha moments"—when I began viewing relationships through the lens of these guiding principles of transformational trust. It happened while participating in a particularly difficult conversation with a coworker that I found challenging to work alongside, someone I definitely considered an adversary.

At that time, I was working as a physician leader in a hospital setting and trying to move the needle on improving physician well-being among my medical staff. It was a daunting task, as burnout was already high and perceived to be rising. There were a number of initiatives that I wanted to implement, and this would require collaboration and greater support from other leaders.

One leader in particular—we'll call him Peter—was critical to the success of my strategy and effort. The problem, I quickly realized, was that I did not have a good working relationship with Peter. In fact, we seemed to be at odds most of the time. We would disagree frequently, and our interactions were tense and uncomfortable. This tension had been present for several months.

Then one day, that aha moment occurred. Peter and I were in a heated debate, and suddenly I realized the disconnect. I did not trust him. I did not have an authentic relationship with him, candor and clarity were not present, and we had no transparency with each other. I also realized that he didn't trust me. *He did not trust me . . . !* That was the understanding that made the lessons come to life. Almost unconsciously I exercised the humility to step back, assess the situation honestly, and take responsibility for the relationship.

So what could I do about it? Admittedly it took some time for me to develop the courage to address this challenging connection. But ultimately, I decided it was critical that I continue to take responsibility for this relationship, seize the opportunity to improve it, lean even more into humility, and be vulnerable.

I reached out to Peter and scheduled an appointment. In our meeting, I shared my regret about the poor quality of our relationship and said I wanted to work on making it a strong one. I discussed my desire for candor and clarity of purpose. I told him I would work on being more present and open-minded in our conversations.

The reality is that this interaction could have gone several ways. He could have questioned my motives and decided he did not have a desire to work on this relationship. He could have demonstrated skepticism and remained defensive. Thankfully, that did not happen.

Peter agreed to work on this relationship and appreciated that I had initiated the conversation. We decided to meet regularly and quickly realized that we had a number of opportunities to work together for the benefit of both of our teams. In time the intentional work we both put into strengthening our connection resulted in strong trust between us. Initially adversaries, we navigated to agnostics when we were not sure how trust was working. After some months, we grew to be allies. And over the years, we emerged as advocates for each other.

When we become intentional about building trust in our relationships, it filters how we act and how we respond to situations. Those who have taken the four-hour training program have noticed this change begins a few days or weeks after learning the transformational trust attributes and guiding principles. We expect your experience will be similar. Once you've taken time to reflect on the attributes and guiding principles, examine how they show up in your relationships and where you might need to make improvements. After that, it will become difficult, if not impossible, to approach relationships without viewing them through the lens of transformational trust. Our research of the program has shown this to be a consistent outcome.

Trust building requires work, focus, and intentionality. But the effort leads to significant rewards.

## The Two Drivers That Steer Trust

Achieving transformational trust in your relationships means that you act on a set of guiding principles every day, aspiring to achieve essential attributes that you will need for people to trust you. From here on we will concentrate on what you need to *do* (daily regular actions) and *be* (in the eyes of others).

Before we dive further into building trust, though, we must first understand two core drivers that form the foundation of whether people trust us or not. At the end of chapter one, you thought of the three people you trust most. What were the words you used to describe these people? We've asked this question in hundreds of training sessions, speeches, and programs and to thousands of people over the past years. Inevitably, we see that the words people use to describe those they trust most fall into two categories:

1. *Emotion*—We are touched by the way people stir our emotions through their sincerity, thoughtfulness, and engagement with us. In our relationships, we feel an emotional connection to the trust we extend or that is extended to us by others.
2. *Experience*—When people demonstrate their competence, consistency, reliability, and integrity over time, those experiences provide the framework of how much we will trust them.

People have an emotional connection with others they trust, as well as an experiential connection. These two ideas each pour into the reservoir of trust, contributing in differing ways and amounts. We have to take both into account when striving to understand why someone trusts or does not trust us.

## Emotion and Experience

Remember, trust is not a one-dimensional quality, it consists of many contributing factors within the two primary drivers of emotion and experience. This is the foundation for how we cultivate the trust that defines our relationships.

We assign different levels of trust in our personal and professional lives, and we trust in different ways.

For instance, you might have strong affection for someone (emotion) and would trust him or her with your deepest, darkest secrets, but you might not ever trust them to do a job for you because they aren't reliable (experience).

Similarly, you may work with someone and know them to be incredibly dependable (experience) but do not feel comfortable enough to share details of your personal life with them (emotion). When you think about people you work with, you may have a high connection with them based on the experience of how well they do a job; however, you may not connect with them emotionally to develop a deeper trust relationship.

*Figure 4.1*

Keep in mind that *emotion* and *experience* influence others' perception of us, as well as our perception of them. Therefore, being aware of both factors is important as we become intentional in building more trust into our relationships.

The question we will address throughout this book is:

*How do you achieve transformational trust—high in BOTH emotion and experience—in your relationships?*

Ultimately, we are striving to build relationships that are productive, fulfilling, and enriching through the trust that is cultivated. The tools we share will help you build both factors effectively, so you have a strong foundation with high levels of both emotional and experiential connections.

## What We Must *Be*

Emerging from the concepts of emotion and experience are the four attributes of transformational trust.

To achieve transformational trust in our relationships, people need to be:

- Trustworthy
- Authentic
- Dependable
- Influential

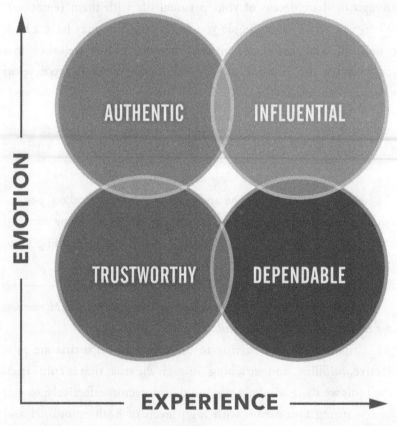

*Figure 4.2*

Coupled with humility, these four attributes together provide a clear path that leads us to transformational trust.

**Trustworthy** (adj)—*worthy of confidence*[28]

At the intersection of emotion and experience, "trustworthy" describes the kind of trust that you have in yourself and the foundation for building trust with others in your life.

**Authentic** (adj)—*worthy of acceptance or belief as conforming to or based on fact; true to one's own personality, spirit, or character*[29]

Aligning with the emotional drivers, this is the kind of trust that solidifies the one-on-one relationship you have with others and provides a solid connection to opening doors and extending relationships beyond your immediate circle.

**Dependable** (adj)—*capable of being trusted or depended on*[30]

Informed by the experience people have, this is the kind of trust others have in you to deliver on your promises, complete a job, and solve problems. It is fostered through consistent communication and is the best defense in crises.

**Influential** (adj)—*exerting or possessing influence*[31]

When trust is earned through the aforementioned attributes, you are expected to use it well. This is the kind of trust that impacts and changes lives and is the trademark of successful and significant leaders in all walks of life and throughout history.[32]

These attributes build on one another to provide a road map for cultivating trust in your relationships and for fortifying trust. They also align with a set of guiding principles and work in tandem with one another to help you achieve transformational trust.

## What We Must *Do*

The guiding principles of transformational trust establish an expectation of personal responsibility in caring for and cultivating relationships with an emphasis on trust. This is the "what you must do" part in your relationships.

To successfully achieve the status of "trusted" and hit the mark on the four attributes of transformational trust, you must adhere to this set of guiding principles to govern your behavior and set priorities in building the kind of trust with others that secures the most productive, profitable, and fulfilling relationships.

**The Guiding Principles** are:

1. Take responsibility for your relationships.
2. Build trust from the inside out.
3. Keep your promises and communicate consistently.
4. Be a good steward of your trust.

## Four Attributes Snapshot Grid

Figure 4.3 provides a snapshot of the model that will be explained in detail in the chapters that follow.

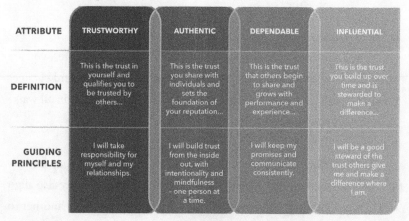

| ATTRIBUTE | TRUSTWORTHY | AUTHENTIC | DEPENDABLE | INFLUENTIAL |
|---|---|---|---|---|
| DEFINITION | This is the trust in yourself and qualifies you to be trusted by others... | This is the trust you share with individuals and sets the foundation of your reputation... | This is the trust that others begin to share and grows with performance and experience... | This is the trust you build up over time and is stewarded to make a difference... |
| GUIDING PRINCIPLES | I will take responsibility for myself and my relationships. | I will build trust from the inside out, with intentionality and mindfulness - one person at a time. | I will keep my promises and communicate consistently. | I will be a good steward of the trust others give me and make a difference where I am. |

*Figure 4.3*

## Reflection

1.  What has experience taught you about your most trusted relationships? What emotions best define trust in your relationships?

2.  Which of the attributes of transformational trust do you feel are most present in your relationships? What steps can you take to strengthen the attributes you have or address the ones you may be lacking?

3.  We've stated that to achieve transformational trust you must work to be trustworthy, which means being more accountable for what you do. How do you feel about this work and responsibility?

# CHAPTER FIVE

# BE TRUSTWORTHY:
## TAKE RESPONSIBILITY
## FOR YOUR RELATIONSHIPS

*"Inaction breeds doubt and fear.*
*Action breeds confidence and courage."*
~Dale Carnegie

ere's an important question: *Do you trust yourself?*

If so, why? And if not, why not? It's worth exploring. A big part of being trustworthy is trusting yourself, which may be the most transformational part of your journey. To achieve personal goals and expectations, being trustworthy is essential. In this chapter we unpack trustworthiness—examining its core aspects and how you achieve it. Trustworthiness is the attribute that aligns with the guiding principle "Take Responsibility for Your Relationships" and starts with your relationship with yourself.

Let's begin with a story of putting trustworthiness to the test.

After many years of studying martial arts, the day came for me (Roy) to test for the rank of third-degree black belt. The final hurdle of the examination was the breaking ceremony. This specific level required me to use my bare hands to knife chop through three clay tiles standing on edge. That is, to use the outside of my hand, cut across my body, and break through the tiles. For this challenge, I needed to focus on generating enough power from my feet and through my body to erupt in my hand as it struck the tiles in precisely the right place to break all three.

I've always enjoyed testing. It's transformational. I especially appreciate the breaking ceremonies, as they provide a unique focus and moment where you must suspend the doubts and fears—and in many cases long-held beliefs—about the physical limitations you have or the perceived durability of the item in front of you. For this test, you have to completely remove and conquer a real fear.

I took my place at the end of a line of anxious students. As I waited for my turn to break, I felt a bit nervous but also confident. I had worked for this day—prepared for it physically, mentally, and spiritually. And now it was time to see if my effort had paid off.

When my turn arrived, I stepped forward and walked toward the station with the clay tiles. Halfway across the floor, my instructor Master David Turnbull intercepted me and said, "Roy, we do not believe that this breaking technique is a true test of your abilities and have something else in mind."

With an outstretched arm, he directed me toward a completely different station. This one had four concrete blocks stacked between two cinder blocks. My eyes grew wide, and my pulse quickened as I realized what he was asking. This was a much greater challenge. Instead of breaking three 1/4-inch tiles, I had to break four two-inch-thick concrete blocks.

I had seen this break done before. It required a palm strike, hammer fist, or elbow strike technique. But I hadn't done it personally. Suddenly, I realized this represented a significant test of trust . . . for both me and my instructors. At that moment I had to ask: Do I trust myself?

This larger question could be broken down into a number of smaller questions:

- Did I commit to my training with integrity?
- Did I have the right attitude to do what was being asked?
- Was I focused on the right thing, right then?
- Had I taken the initiative to learn, teach, and grow?
- Did I have the right insights to complete the task?
- Would I persevere when it got difficult?
- Did I have a vision for reaching the next level?

I needed to address all these questions on a conscious and subconscious level in order to succeed in the breaking ceremony.

Over the next few minutes, my master and grandmaster came over, helped me take measure of the break, worked on the placement of my feet, and offered a few tips for my success. They fed into my confidence that had now grown, despite the initial shock of the new expectation. But ultimately, I had to trust myself to complete the task.

I decided to use a palm strike. I stepped up to the blocks, took two deep breaths, did a slow practice of the angle and flow of the strike. Then, on the third breath, I released the blow with everything I had in me. And my hand shattered . . . No, wait, just kidding. Actually, my hand went through all four blocks with little or no apparent resistance. The concrete seemed to explode.

Completing the test for a third-degree black belt answered that question for me that I'd asked earlier: Do I trust myself?

What about you? How do you answer this question? How have you tested this idea in your life?

## Trusting Yourself

We all want to BELIEVE we are trustworthy, but how can we be sure if we really are? As previously stated, trustworthiness begins with trusting yourself. (If you don't trust yourself, others will find it difficult to trust you.) It requires a deep understanding of who you are and a commitment to a set of inner values that lead to outward actions.

Many people confuse the words "trustworthy" and "trusted." The difference is important, so let's take a look at how to distinguish between the two: **Trustworthiness is earning the right to be trusted**.

Trustworthiness is about who you are as a person on the inside (your values and standards). This translates to outward actions (your behaviors and performance), which give others (as well as yourself) tangible reasons to trust you. We might visualize it this way:

**Inner Commitment + Outward Actions = Trustworthiness**

When I approached the concrete blocks for the testing, I had an inner commitment. But it wasn't until I acted on that commitment and completed the concrete break (an outward action) that I proved to myself I was trustworthy.

An inner commitment to live by a set of values will lead you to behaviors that demonstrate your commitment to ethics, consistency, and performance. Trusting yourself is essential as you set out to achieve your most significant goals and aspirations. If you set a goal to get into shape, you have to trust yourself to eat properly, exercise, get enough rest, and invest time in planning for success. If you want to start a business, you will need to trust yourself to do the work, set the budget, build the plan, and have the discipline to execute it effectively.

In her TED Talk "What We Don't Understand about Trust,"[33] philosopher Onora O'Neill said, "Trust is the response. Trustworthiness is what we have to judge," citing the distinct difference between the two. Here's another way to think of it:

> **Trustworthiness is the kind of trust
> you have in yourself, which lays the
> foundation for building trust with others.**

Trustworthiness, then, is determined by a set of characteristics or qualities that are daily reflected in your beliefs, ideas, and actions. What are these internal characteristics that we should believe and live by? Well, there are many excellent personal values that each of us could choose. However, in our study and experience, eight characteristics kept rising to the surface. Each of these characteristics lays the groundwork for the next, to help you achieve trustworthiness and thereby earn the right for people to trust you.

Earlier in the book, we introduced the four attributes of trust along with the four guiding principles that align with them. Let's analyze the first of the four attributes and its corresponding guiding principle.

## Transformational Trust Attribute: Trustworthy

Guiding Principle: Take Responsibility for Your Relationships

Trustworthiness sits at the axis of emotion and experience. It is the kind of trust that you have in yourself, and your foundation for building trust with others. *(Figure 5.1)*

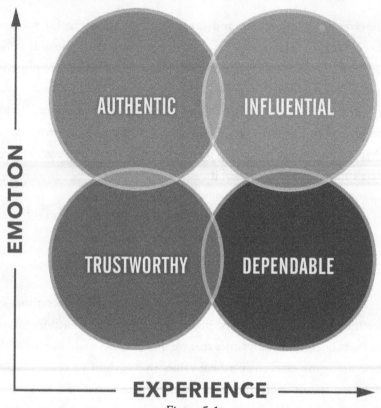

*Figure 5.1*

In the world we live in, people are often quick to dismiss their responsibility in relationships. This is especially true when frustration, confrontation, or anger flare up. Have you ever heard someone proclaim, "Well, if he has a problem with me, he can come down here and tell me about it!"? That approach, or some similar sentiment, is rarely the first step toward a solution. If the speaker is focused almost entirely on their own feelings, they are likely not prepared to take responsibility for the relationship by being open to listening to the other person's point of view.

As we noted earlier, being humble is key because it naturally puts a greater focus on the quality of our relationships. It makes us more willing to listen, understand, and value another person's point of view. And, even if we have been wronged, those who are humble heal sooner, learn more, and positively affect others with their responses. This, in turn, opens the door to increasing levels of trust.

Of course, there are no guarantees when you make yourself vulnerable by taking responsibility for trust. Trust can die as easily as thrive due to any number of issues outside your immediate control. Just because you choose to take responsibility for relationships doesn't mean the other person will. Trust is based on another's perceptions and is formed from his or her emotions and experience with you.

However, once you take a significant step to improve a relationship, you put into motion a number of positive efforts. These can impact both the person you're reaching out to as well as others who will observe and appreciate your efforts.

Choice is powerful, and taking responsibility is a transformational choice. Think of the impact when you say, "I own this relationship, and I take full responsibility for cultivating trust with this person or with that group of people." Others will act differently, people around you will notice, and you will see the results of increasing trust from both the primary engagement and secondary channels.

## Lead with Trust

Once we tune in to the frequency of others' needs, we can much more easily open the doors to solve problems, develop productive engagements, and harness loyalty. Don't let trust be a passing thought or simply a nice idea. Focus on trust as the most important outcome in all engagements. Regardless of whom you engage, what situation you may be facing, or where you find yourself, you must *always* intentionally work to establish and maintain trust. Each word or action should be measured as to whether it will enhance or take away from your ability to build trust. Everything you do contributes to or diminishes the capacity of others to trust you.

When you are intentional about building trust, you will be more mindful of your words and actions, filtering them to ensure you are constantly moving toward stronger trust. Intentionality sets a powerful benchmark for our behavior.

## Risk and Fear

Intentional trust building involves both risk and fear. You are making yourself more vulnerable, and risking failure. But failing when you are striving to be virtuous is always better than succeeding at doing nothing. As you strengthen your trust in yourself, you can more readily lean into vulnerability and open the door to taking responsibility for your relationships. In *The Power of Vulnerability*, Brené Brown says, "Vulnerability is our most accurate measure of courage."

The bracelet story in chapter one reminds us that we will fail . . . perhaps often and unwittingly. Yet even failure can yield a positive outcome if we choose to intentionally follow a path of rebuilding trust in the broken relationship.

Fear is the enemy of trust and holds us back from restoring trust with others and fostering the most fulfilling relationships. We defeat fear with action. By taking responsibility for breaches of trust, you will begin to see how the risks you take yield rewards, transforming your relationships as well as your soul. Over time, you will become fearless in pursuing trust.

## Eight Characteristics of Trustworthiness

Think of this list of trustworthy characteristics as a series of steps toward trusting yourself and achieving trustworthiness. Each of them builds on and works in concert with the others.

Your commitment to the eight qualities of trustworthiness is important in setting a firm foundation for fostering and strengthening relationships. Being intentional in building each of these into your life and your work is essential.

## 1. Integrity
*Have I acted with the highest degree of integrity in my interaction with others?*

The characteristic perhaps most associated with trustworthiness is integrity. Think of someone you trust. Why do you trust them? Chances are, you trust that person because he or she is a person of integrity. Integrity is a word commonly used—especially in business settings. But what does it actually mean?

**Integrity** (n)—*firm adherence to a code of especially moral or artistic values: INCORRUPTIBILITY*[34]

How do you demonstrate this characteristic?
- **Keep Promises** – Do what you say you will do. People of integrity act honestly and admit mistakes. Integrity means saying "no" to shortcuts and unethical efforts as much as it means saying "yes" to doing something the right way, regardless of difficulty.
- **Speak Truth** – Tell the truth, candidly but not rudely. Let others clearly understand your position without being misleading or giving a wrong impression.
- **Do Right** – Do the right thing even when no one is around to see you. Take action whether it's expected or not. Some may use this as the common definition of character. We suggest expanding on this. Do the right thing when no one is looking, and also when everyone is looking. Others will take note of your decisions and behaviors, and this can carry significant influence.

## 2. Attitude
*Is my attitude optimistic and appropriate for the task at hand?*

**Attitude** (n)—*a mental position with regard to a fact or state*[35]

Your attitude will dictate how someone interprets your reactions, framing their belief about you. Controlling your attitude can be the greatest advantage you have in dealing with difficult situations or seeing past the conflict to find a solution.

Research continues to show us that attitude has far more influence in our success than any other contributing factor. An article in *Forbes* entitled "Why Attitude Is More Important Than IQ" cites a Stanford study by Dr. Carol Dweck.

> *Psychologist Carol Dweck has spent her entire career studying attitude and performance, and her latest study shows that your attitude is a better predictor of your success than your IQ.*[36]

Your attitude is often the ONLY thing you have control of in certain situations. So many stories of success and achievement find their catalyst in the attitude of the protagonist in the story. A great attitude in the face of a challenge will produce better outcomes from you and those around you.

One of the most powerful illustrations of how attitude shapes people's behavior and outcomes can be found in the writings of Viktor Frankl. In his acclaimed book *Man's Search for Meaning*, Frankl provides a firsthand account of his time in a concentration camp and how he survived by taking control of his attitude in the midst of horrific suffering:

> *Everything can be taken from a man but one thing: the last of human freedoms—to choose one's attitude in any given set of circumstances, to choose one's own way.*[37]

John Maxwell, renowned leader in business and ministry, says in his book, *The Difference Maker*:

> *Your attitude colors every aspect of your life. It is like the mind's paintbrush.*[38]

Attitude is contagious—and it is always transformational. One of the ways we can frame our attitude is by approaching it from the perspective of gratitude. Numerous studies have described with empirical evidence the benefit of practicing gratitude. Gratitude is a natural mood booster and antidepressant. It enhances empathy and self-esteem. It has physical benefits of creating a stronger immune system, improving sleep quality, and lowering blood pressure. It also serves to strengthen social bonds and friendships.

One of the most well-known studies, conducted by Martin Seligman and colleagues, monitored participants who practiced an exercise called "Three Good Things." In the study, participants were instructed to write each evening three things that went well that day. They were also told to reflect on the causes of these good things. Participants continued this exercise every day for a week. The researchers identified that this simple daily exercise had a significant impact on improving well-being and reducing depression. Additionally, participants who continued with this exercise beyond the first week were found to have increased happiness for up to six months and decreased symptoms of depression for up to three months after the intervention.[39]

There are real world applications of this exercise. The ease and simplicity of it make it a useful tool for anyone to try. We considered this as we broached the issue of rising burnout in emergency medicine physicians and allied health professionals.

We surveyed twenty-five emergency medicine clinicians at a busy tertiary care hospital. Participants were asked to complete a burnout assessment from Duke University where the highest score on the burnout scale was 25.[40] The clinical staff surveyed had an average score of 23. To identify the possible impact of intentional gratitude on reducing burnout and improving overall physician well-being, participants were asked to complete the Three Good Things exercise for one week.

The benefits of and practice of intentional gratitude were reviewed with the participants. A text reminder that included all the clinicians was sent at 9:00 p.m. each night for one week, encouraging them to journal their three good things from the day with a reflection of the cause.

At the end of the week, participants revealed the results they saw in themselves as well as in their families. Many commented on the frame shift they observed. Where they previously had felt inclined to see things negatively and feared a bad outcome, they now saw events that occurred in a positive light. Several included their families in the exercise and noted that it had become a nightly family ritual. Many clinicians expressed their continued commitment to the practice of gratitude.

Improving our attitude takes intentionality. We are in control of how we react to our circumstances. Habits such as practicing gratitude prepare us to better respond to our environment in a productive manner.

## 3. Focus

*Am I focused on the most important thing right now?*

Trustworthy people understand what's most important and stay on task to complete it. This is essential in our pursuit of personal transformation, our work with our teams, our engagement with customers, and our familial responsibilities. Understanding the priorities and building in the systems or discipline to keep these priorities in focus reflect our commitment to ourselves and those for whom we are responsible.

Remember that people know when you don't have their priorities in mind. I (Roy) recall sitting in my office the first day I began my work at Consensus Communications, a public relations firm. My client had a strong presence and ran a remarkable business. (I would find myself learning much from him in our future meetings.) On this day, he made an incredibly salient point related to customer expectations and the importance of focus. He said, "There are so many ways to succeed in the work we do. I will tell you, though, there is one thing that I deem to be a failure. It's when someone comes into the meeting, puts the agenda on the table, and the item that I feel is most important doesn't show up until number five or six." His observation may be one of the clearest examples of how one's focus—or lack of it—can affect their trustworthiness.

As a consumer, when are you most likely to have a good experience with an organization? It's probably when they focus on your needs and outcomes. We appreciate this in our personal relationships as well. People are drawn to those who address their most important issues. Focus enables presence and feeds authenticity. It's impossible to be present if you are unable to focus on who is in front of you right now.

## 4. Initiative
*Do I take initiative to solve problems?*

This is where we begin to see the actions that define trustworthiness. Trustworthy people don't wait for others to act. A trustworthy person will take the initiative and move on the issue at hand. They are problem solvers.

If you've set a goal to lose weight (who hasn't?), nothing will happen until you change your eating, begin to exercise, and/or improve your rest. The best plans are useless unless you take steps to activate them.

How do you feel when you act, as opposed to when you don't? It's not a hard question. We usually feel disappointed, because we know that change only happens the way we want it to, when we move on the plans we make.

What's great about initiative is that it doesn't have to be big to be strong. Like the old maxim says, "Every journey begins with one step." That one step is the initiative. When one person acts, it makes it easier for others to do so as well. Pretty soon, a large group of people is engaged in an issue or important work, and everyone benefits from the outcome. Within this sphere of action we find other powerful ideas that feed trustworthiness, like vulnerability and risk.

Earlier in this chapter we mentioned that we put ourselves at risk when we are vulnerable. However, transformational trust cannot be present in our relationships without vulnerability, which stems from initiative. Someone has to "break the ice" and open the conversation. Because we love Brené Brown's perspective on vulnerability, here is one more powerful quote from her book *The Gifts of Imperfection*:

> *We cultivate love when we allow our most vulnerable and powerful selves to be deeply seen and known, and when we honor the spiritual connection that grows from that offering with trust, respect, kindness, and affection.*[41]

Initiative opens the door to reconciliation. Someone must be willing to take that first step to be humble, recognize that in a broken relationship both parties may have contributed to the issues, and be willing to take ownership of their part. Initiative drives us to fix the things that are broken in relationships.

## 5. Insight
*How am I gaining greater insight and wisdom?*

The most trustworthy people are lifelong learners, constantly striving for improvement and have a sense of personal accountability for their own development. This doesn't mean you are always in school; however, it does mean that you make time to learn new things and engage with others.

By taking some simple steps, you can build your knowledge and cultivate wisdom. The first may be to make time to read more. Now, with audiobooks, you can be learning and growing while driving in your car or out on a walk. Opening yourself up to new ideas through reading also provides you with the ability to learn shortcuts through other people's stories and experiences.

Another way to gain insight is through mentorship. Mentors help bring ideas to life and provide feedback on those ideas. They also can help us see beyond the curves of life through their experiences and perspective, so we might learn from their mistakes and trials. Some choose mentors or coaches for specific life challenges in areas such as work, leadership, health and fitness, and spirituality.

Commit to lifelong learning.

*A Mentorship Rooted in Relationships*

One reason I (Roy) am such a strong believer in mentorships is that I was blessed with a team of remarkable mentors, and I have firsthand experience of the valuable insights and extraordinary trust relationships that can develop from strong mentorships.

As a senior in college, I needed an internship to complete my studies in public relations. I was serving as student body president and was making some good contacts in the community. I had a professor who took a great interest in me and provided the introduction that defined my career.

Frank Stansbury, a director for the Coca-Cola corporation, ran the American Pavilion at EPCOT. He was also an adjunct professor at UCF and taught public relations campaigns. Frank, who was—and still is—one of the very best public relations practitioners, had a direct style in his teaching. You always knew where you stood with him.

I found out on my first day in Frank's class just how direct and insightful he was. I was running late, coming from a fraternity softball game where I had gotten quite dirty and even had an open wound on my leg from sliding into home plate. As I attempted to enter class unobserved, Frank called me out. "Ladies and gentlemen, let me introduce you to your student body president, Mr. Roy Reid . . . thank you for joining us tonight, Mr. Reid . . . and thank you for taking time to clean up . . . is that blood on your leg?" I knew right away; Frank and I were going to get along just fine.

Frank made himself available to anyone who made the effort to connect. About halfway through the semester, Frank got a call from Roger Pynn, who ran one of the largest PR firms in Orlando. Roger was looking for intern candidates for one of his clients. Frank suggested me.

Roger invited me to meet with Randy Berridge, AT&T's public relations director for central and north Florida. I met Randy and was selected. I began my internship with Randy Berridge in 1988, and—as I like to tell people—it's going strong today.

On the first day, Randy laid out two ideas that have become woven into my professional DNA. First, he made clear that mentoring relationships are two-way. I would have three mentors between himself, Roger, and Frank. But we would all benefit together. We would learn from each other in everything we did. Randy's second point was that regardless of whatever I chose to do in my career, my network of relationships would be the most valuable asset in my life. I needed to take care of my network and manage it carefully. Those two lessons were branded into my consciousness during that internship and in the years that followed.

I have never made a career move without at least one conversation with Randy. And there have been times when a call from Randy, Roger, or Frank to a potential employer of mine would finalize the deal on me getting hired.

I continue to seek out mentors in the places where I want to grow and am eternally grateful for the example these three men set for me in the early and formative stages of my career. They entrusted me with their time and energy, with the expectation that I would return the favor by mentoring the young people who would follow me. Mentors are the most efficient way to gain the insight that will set you apart and help you become more trustworthy.

## 6. Perseverance
*Do I have the perseverance to struggle through the difficult times?*

Trustworthy people do not cut and run when things get tough. This is important for us in our own struggles as well as how we show up to support others. Think about the most important goals you've set out to accomplish in your life. Were there difficult parts to achieving success? If you had not stuck with your plan during that time, would you have achieved the goal?

We like to describe perseverance as an emotional muscle that gets stronger the more you work it. And you work this muscle by taking on challenging opportunities. Like beginning an exercise program, or more specifically, lifting weights, the challenge you may take on early to develop the "perseverance muscle" might be smaller, more manageable. But as you achieve a succession of these smaller goals, that muscle becomes stronger and able to handle weightier (yes we did) or more difficult challenges.

To persevere may also mean that we ask for help. To trust in ourselves means we understand and are honest with ourselves about our strengths, and we are humble enough (remember the bracelet) to seek support for dealing with difficult situations. And, if we've engaged the mentors discussed above, we have guides with experience to help us navigate uncharted waters.

Perseverance is also a quality we must have in supporting and working with others. It's in the midst of a challenge when we discover ourselves and learn what we're truly capable of. When we are pouring our effort into helping someone else navigate the storm, there is an even greater benefit, because we gain energy from the shared effort. Think about a moment when you jumped in to help someone with a problem, or a time when you were part of a team that had an overwhelming objective to achieve. When you are in sync with others, working together for a common goal, everyone gains from the experience.

## 7. Excellence

*Have I delivered my best work first?*

American historian and philosopher Will Durant said, "We are what we repeatedly do. Excellence, then, is not an act, but a habit." The most trustworthy people have a habit of excellence. They believe, "If a job is worth doing, it's worth doing right."

When someone gives you something to work on, it's easy to think of it as one more thing on your to-do list. However, that task may be the most important thing on *their* list, and they trusted you enough to do it! This kind of shift in thinking—which stems from your integrity and attitude (see how these things all connect?)—should make a significant difference in how you approach work. People will notice your output and quality of work, and it will influence them emotionally and experientially, feeding their perception of your trustworthiness.

Deliver excellence in all that you do. When you commit to something, your best effort is required to fulfill your commitment to be trustworthy in serving others.

## 8. Vision

*Is my vision driven by something bigger than myself?*

The best companies operate with a vision, purpose, or mission that defines something bigger than just the transactional aspects of the business. At AdventHealth, where we have both worked for many years, the mission is "Extending the Healing Ministry of Christ." This mission sets the agenda for both what the organization does and how they do it, thereby shaping the culture of the company. The mission informs the vision (where the organization is planning to go) as well as the service standards (how employees are expected to treat one another, patients, consumers, and the community).

One of the most respected brands is Chick-fil-A, which operates with the purpose "To glorify God by being a faithful steward of all that is entrusted to us. To have a positive influence on all who come in contact with Chick-fil-A." As the founder, S. Truett Cathy, put it, "Most people think we are in the chicken business, but we're not. We are in the people business." The legacy of his comments is clearly articulated in the company purpose, and it's what drives everything people who work for Chick-fil-A do, from the corporate support team to the local restaurant staff. Chick-fil-A employees are taught to respond with, "My pleasure" because their role is to serve and give customers the best experience.

What drives and inspires you to do what you do? In chapter six, when we explore authenticity, we will discuss clarity of purpose. Finding that clarity begins with having a vision for something bigger than yourself. Rick Warren writes:

*The more you lead a self-focused life, the more you're prone to discouragement. Every time you forget that it's not about you, you're going to get prideful or fearful or bitter. Those feelings will always lead to discouragement because they keep you focused on yourself.*

## Steps for Building Trustworthiness

To further illustrate the importance of the eight characteristics of trustworthiness and how they build upon each other, let's return to Roy's martial arts training.

Martial arts are often associated with the idea of combat. While that certainly is an element of martial arts, in my experience they are transformational arts of physical, intellectual, and spiritual exercises that people practice for many reasons, including self-defense, fitness, and personal development, as well as for competition and entertainment.

Even if you aren't familiar with disciplined sport, perhaps you have heard about a martial arts student gaining a black belt. In martial arts, a black belt means the practitioner has earned a certain significant standing or achieved particular milestones in the class. This qualification is gained through a process of training, teaching, and testing over a period of time. Typically, an individual begins with a white belt and works up through a series of qualifications. In the process of obtaining a black belt, the practitioner wears a number of other different colored belts in a prescribed succession to signal their level of growth. What sets the black belt apart is an understanding and commitment to constantly practice the fundamentals and work to perfect them in their art.

The process of moving from a white belt to a black belt in martial arts is a fitting metaphor for the journey many of us must go through in discovering and mastering transformational trust. In developing the framework for trustworthiness, that same idea is reflected—we must begin with a firm foundation, grow through a series of tests, and continually strive to improve how we live out these attributes each day. Our job is to constantly work to perfect these ideas in our lives, and in time, people will say that we have mastered them.

A common misconception about a black belt is that the achievement is the final destination. In actuality, the black belt is the beginning of the journey for the true martial artist, as it opens up the opportunity for a deep study and understanding of the art. Similarly, trustworthiness opens the door for transformational trust in our relationships.

One way to visualize these eight characteristics of trustworthiness is as a progression of belts you receive as you become more proficient in exercising each of them in your life.

## Belts of Trustworthiness

1. *Integrity* – *Commit to personal honor and honesty.*
2. *Attitude* – *Maintain a positive outlook.*

3. **Focus** – *Concentrate on the important issues.*

4. **Initiative** – *Take action and the lead in solving problems.*

5. **Insight** – *Dedicate yourself to lifelong learning to gain understanding to help others.*

6. **Perseverance** – *Determine to never quit, and push through when things get difficult.*

7. **Excellence** – *Strive to produce high-quality work.*

8. **Vision** – *Commit to something bigger than yourself, incorporate empathy, and create an optimistic picture of the future.*

Again, these eight characteristics of trustworthiness speak to the person you are on the inside (your values and standards), and they translate into outward actions (your behaviors and performance) that give others tangible reasons to trust you. And before you can expect others to trust you, you must believe that you are trustworthy, live by these characteristics, and learn to trust yourself.

## Reflection

1. Which of the eight characteristics of trustworthy behavior do you feel is your strongest? Why?

2. Does the idea of building trust with current agnostics or adversaries scare you? What are the potential outcomes of showing vulnerability?

3. Which of the eight characteristics of trustworthiness do you value most in others? Why?

# CHAPTER SIX

# BE AUTHENTIC:
# *BUILD TRUST FROM THE INSIDE OUT*

*"Authenticity is a collection of choices that we have to make every day. It's about the choice to show up and be real. The choice to be honest. The choice to let our true selves be seen."*
~Brené Brown

I n business and professional relationships, we all need people we can trust. Trustworthy people are not perfect. They aren't people who never make a mistake. But they are authentic people willing to cultivate candor and listen to honest, respectful feedback and humbly do whatever it takes to rebuild broken trust in relationships.

In *The Hidden Power of Relentless Stewardship*, author Don Jernigan wrote:

*Trust is the coin of the realm. In many ways, trust is like money. You can spend it, you can bank it, or you can invest it. And if you are not careful, through foolish choices you can totally drain your account of it.*[42]

It's a powerful way to think about trust. If, like money, trust is not handled wisely, it may be lost quickly and permanently. To avoid that happening to you, learn the value of being authentic and cultivating candor in your relationships.

## Transformational Trust Attribute: Authentic

Guiding Principle: Build Trust from the Inside Out

"Authentic" is our second attribute, and it is anchored on the emotional axis. It is the foundation for our most intimate and lasting friendships. We experience authenticity in people when we sense that they are sincere in their interactions.

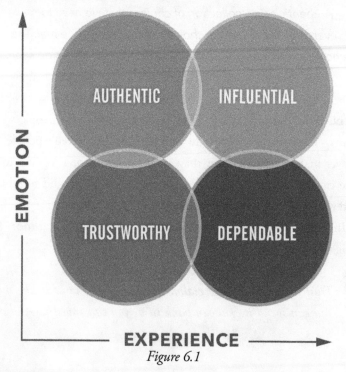

*Figure 6.1*

Ask yourself these questions: What does sincerity look and feel like to me? Am I authentic with others?

Authenticity is a component of trust which solidifies your relationship with others. It creates a solid connection, opening doors and extending lines of communication beyond your immediate circle. Being authentic is so important that we suggest you challenge yourself in this area *before* expecting others to trust you.

## Building Trust Circles

Trust and authenticity start from within. We have to build them from the inside out. We must trust ourselves first before we can create trusting relationships with others. Once we do, we can begin to form bonds with those closest to us and, ultimately, with those in our workplaces and in our communities. Figure 6.2 illustrates the inside-out process that orders how we build trust:

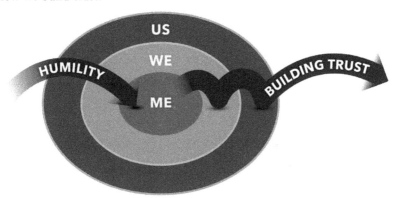

*Figure 6.2*

- **Me (personal trust)** – the work we must do within our self to establish trust in ourselves and qualify to earn trust from others
- **We (family and friends)** – the intimate personal relationships reflected in those with family and friends
- **Us (colleagues, customers, boss, or groups)** – the daily interactions in the places we live and work

Personal growth requires humble, honest self-reflection. Remember the story of the bead bracelet in chapter 1? It illustrated how humility and self-awareness were vital for repairing a breach of trust.

Humility is the active agent that tells us it's essential to go back to "me" to understand what must be. Remember, you can't change anyone but yourself. But if you build your authenticity and trustworthiness from within, these qualities will become evident to others and will positively affect your efforts to widen your trust circles.

## Worthy, Real, and Sincere

What exactly does it mean to be "authentic"? First, it means "being worthy of acceptance or belief as conforming to or based on fact" (e.g. *paints an authentic picture of our society*). It can also mean "conforming to an original so as to reproduce essential features" (e.g. *an authentic reproduction of a colonial farmhouse*) or "made or done the same way as an original" (e.g. *authentic Mexican fare*). Authenticity can also mean "not false or imitation: real, actual" (e.g. *an authentic cockney accent*). Finally, it can also mean "being true to one's own personality, spirit, or character is sincere and authentic with no pretensions" (e.g. *I am most authentic when with my best friend*).[43]

**"Worthy of acceptance"** – As we move through the achievement of trustworthiness, people see something in our actions, our character, and our spirit that allows them to accept or embrace a relationship with us.

**"Real"** – This quality requires vulnerability and for us to let people see who we really are. If we have not yet achieved a trust in ourselves (trustworthiness), how can we be real?

**"Character is sincere"** – Meeting up with sincerity warms our spirit. This truly is the height of connecting with people because it conveys to them that we value them and want to be engaged.

To build transformational trust with others, look within yourself, your organization, and the aspects of life within your control and live out the characteristics of trustworthiness discussed in the previous chapters. Then you can begin to open up and invite—or be invited into—trusting relationships with others. Authenticity allows us first to trust ourselves then to widen our trust circles.

## Six Essential Ingredients for an Authentic Relationship

Understanding the definition of authenticity, let's consider how we leverage essential ingredients in developing relationships with others to optimize the potential for strong trust to be present. Authentic relationships require clarity of purpose, respect for each other, presence, candor between individuals, and forgiveness when a wrongdoing occurs. The ultimate manifestation of these elements results in transparency. Let's take a deeper look at each of these ingredients to better understand where opportunities lie while also reflecting on which are currently our strengths.

### 1. Clarify Purpose

A water bearer in India had two large pots. One hung on each end of a pole, which he carried across his neck. One of the pots had a crack in it, and the other was perfect. The perfect pot always delivered a full portion of water at the end of the long walk from the stream to the master's house, while the cracked pot arrived only half full. For two years this went on daily, with the bearer delivering only one and a half pots of water to his master's house.

The perfect pot was proud of its accomplishments, flawless to the means for which it was made. But the poor cracked pot was ashamed of its imperfection and miserable that it was able to accomplish only half of what it had been made to do. After two years of what it perceived to be a bitter failure, it spoke to the water bearer one day by the stream.

"I am ashamed of myself, and I want to apologize to you."

"Why?" asked the bearer. "What are you ashamed of?"

"I have been able, for these past two years, to deliver only half my load because this crack in my side causes water to leak out all the way back to your master's house. Because of my flaws, you have to do all of this work, and you don't get full value from your efforts," the pot said.

The water bearer felt sorry for the old, cracked pot, and in his compassion he said, "As we return to the master's house, I want you to notice the lovely flowers along the path."

Indeed, as they went up the hill, the old, cracked pot took notice of the sun warming the beautiful wildflowers on the side of the path, and this cheered it some. But at the end of the trail, it still felt bad because it had leaked out half its load, and so again it apologized to the bearer for its failure.

The bearer said to the pot, "Did you notice that there were flowers only on your side of your path, but not on the other pot's side? That's because I have always known about your flaw, and I took advantage of it. I planted flower seeds on your side of the path, and every day while we walked back from the stream, you've watered them. For two years I have been able to pick these pretty flowers to decorate my master's table. Without you being just the way you are, he would not have this beauty to grace his house."

When left only to its own view, the pot believed it was a failure. Only when the water bearer pointed out the beauty the broken vessel was contributing did its outlook and sense of meaning transform. We too have a higher calling than we may realize, though we cannot see it when we concentrate on our imperfections. We can only see our true purpose when we focus on something other than ourselves.

Clarity is an essential element of trust and the first principle of authenticity. We must find our purpose and help others around us find their purpose as well. People who possess this clarity are far more efficient and effective in their work, and generally make better decisions than those without it. Purpose also helps people to stay focused on the big picture and not let issues like personality, business perspectives, or background issues impede them from working with or helping others.

Consider how clarity of purpose can help shape your perspective in your personal and professional relationships. Knowing your purpose provides clarity and focus. Knowing your purpose helps to remove barriers to working with others. Knowing your purpose helps to provide direction. Knowing your purpose creates a consistency in behavior and ideas.

Authenticity requires clarity. Find your purpose, and clarity is the result.

## 2. Always Show Respect

The key to managing relationships is to always show respect. This is not to say that you have to agree with everyone, nor should you reward bad behavior. What is required is to treat people with dignity and respect in every situation. We've probably all heard of the Golden Rule. In only a few words, it summarizes what it means to show respect: "Do unto others as you would have them do unto you."[44] Apply these words as you interact with people, and you will do well!

Life presents any number of conflicts between people, but that doesn't mean that you have to sacrifice respect. Respect provides you a license to make your case, advance your ideas, return for more opportunities, and earn trust.

One doesn't have to always agree with others (it is naïve to believe you will), so work hard to discover similar ground from which you can communicate. Respect contributes to understanding, especially in conflict.

Another method of testing yourself (or others) is called the waiter rule. The idea is that the way a person treats a waiter at a restaurant reveals their true character. Ideally, we should treat all people with dignity, no matter their social status, position, or their ability to benefit us. Some companies place so much importance on this concept that, in hiring new personnel, the CEO always checks with their receptionist after interviewing a job candidate to find out how the potential employee behaved toward them. If the candidate hasn't shown respect and dignity to the receptionist, the CEO won't hire them.[45]

The foundation of respect is being considerate of other people and their feelings. Encourage those around you, remembering that we're all struggling with difficulties. Freely give praise, and congratulate others for their accomplishments. Be ready to lend a hand, and remember to sincerely thank others who help you.

One of the most powerful ways to show respect is to master the art of *active listening*. Active listening shows respect, opens doors, and builds authenticity.

Being a great listener doesn't come naturally to most of us. It requires intentionality and focus. Want to become a better, more active listener? Start by putting down the cell phone, turning away from the computer screen, and eliminating other distractions. Give the other person your undivided attention. This is also a way to show respect. Thoughtfully approach the person who wants to engage you in conversation.

Let's get even more granular. As we list these specific techniques, think of recent interactions you have engaged in and consider whether you practiced the following behaviors consistently:

- Faced the person speaking to you and maintained eye contact
- Used facial expressions appropriate to the conversation to show the other person you understood them and what they were saying
- Focused on what was being said (it's often easy to let your mind wander and only hear half of a conversation)
- Listened—without judging—to understand the other person's idea, not to respond
- Asked questions to indicate you were listening and to clarify points
- Didn't interrupt the other person

Just as it is important that we listen and engage with others, *how* we say something is as critical as *what* we say. Body language conveys more than words do. In his book *Silent Messages*, Dr. Albert Mehrabian found that people receive information in the following ways: 55 percent of what we learn from others comes from their body language, 38 percent comes from their tone of voice, and only 7 percent comes from the words they speak.[46]

## 3. Be Present in Your Relationships

You can't build an authentic relationship if you are never there. Presence is a required investment of time and engagement. People want and need face-to-face interaction to feel the realness and sincerity of your effort. Today, it is too easy to rely on other, less personal forms of communication. We overuse email, text messaging, and social media and consider this engagement a reasonable substitute for personal interaction. We are fooling ourselves.

As a physician, I (Omayra) try to demonstrate presence in my daily interactions with patients. In the emergency department, it is easy for staff to seem rushed, and when we do, we lose the patient's perception that we are present. Simple actions that we try to consistently use to ensure our mindful presence include touching the patient (e.g. shaking their hand or patting their shoulder), introducing everyone in the room when we first enter, and letting patients talk uninterrupted for at least two minutes. One study in the *Journal of the American Medical Association* showed that the majority of medical providers interrupted patients after only twenty-three seconds![47]

Sitting at a patient's bedside is another important aspect of being present. One particular study of 120 adult postoperative inpatients admitted for elective spine surgery found that having a medical professional simply sit down at the bedside increased the patient's perception of time spent by five times the actual amount.[48]

## 4. Cultivate Candor

If you've heard the word candor before, you probably associate it with other words like "direct," "blunt," and "outspoken." While these words capture some aspect of "candor," there's more to the concept than being straightforward with people.

Speaking candidly involves two equally important traits: being truthful and being respectful. Telling someone the truth can be difficult at times. Telling it in a disrespectful way can be alienating and pointless. This is why speaking with candor must include the component of respect.

Early in my career, I (Roy) was invited to sit on the board of a community bank. This was a real honor, and I was excited to serve. I happened to get my first-ever smartphone the week of my initial bank board meeting. With instant access to emails and text, I saw the new phone as a miraculous way to improve communication and client relations.

Almost immediately after the board meeting began, one of my clients emailed me with an issue. With my new technology in hand, I quickly responded and figured I had fixed the problem. I was wrong. Over the course of the next hour, I "subtly" sent and received emails until the issue was resolved. The whole time, I tried to pay attention to what was going on in the meeting. I thought I succeeded in doing two things at once.

When I returned to my office, my account executive, Hue Lien, approached me and asked how the bank meeting had gone.

"It was great," I said.

"How do you know?" she replied. She spoke respectfully, but I could tell from her body language she had something difficult to tell me.

"Someone called me and shared that you were totally checked out," Hue Lien said. "According to this person, you didn't participate in the discussions, seemed preoccupied with your phone, and made zero contributions to the meeting."

I could have answered indignantly, but in my heart, I knew a humble response was the right one. I had a blind spot, and Hue Lien had spoken with candor to point it out to me. I needed to check myself and see what I could to rebuild the trust I'd broken.

I thanked Hue Lien for talking candidly with me about my blind spot. I then called members of the board, apologized for my actions, and assured them I would be fully present at future board meetings. Then, I kept that promise.

A few years later, one of the board members, who also served as CEO for a hospital, needed someone to help manage a crisis. He called and hired me on the spot for a job that would bring hundreds of thousands of dollars to my company. If his initial impression of me as a distracted, unengaged person had remained unchanged—without the apology and follow-up— I'm convinced he would never have considered me for his work.

That is the value of welcoming candor and information about your blind spots. It allows you to transform potentially disastrous situations into good ones.

Speaking with candor may be even more difficult than accepting it. It's tempting to avoid uncomfortable conversations—especially with people in positions of authority. (This is why it's vital for leadership to empower its employees to "speak truth to power" in a way that can build a culture of ethical behavior and trust.) But you must face those tough conversations and uncomfortable realities. As you do, remember that you're tackling issues, not people. Whether speaking with your spouse, child, or colleague, be frank but respectful. Direct, but kind. Your message should neither be watered and weak, nor vicious and cruel. Take a deep breath, muster your courage, and start that difficult conversation.

## Candor Is the Antidote to Self-Deception

Did you know it is possible to lie to yourself? Or, at least, it is possible to avoid the truth. This is a form of self-deception, and it can cause great difficulty for you personally and professionally. If you do not assess the world around you with clarity and honesty, you may harbor unrealistic expectations—which can cause you to make poor decisions.

In his book *Good to Great*, Jim Collins highlights the importance of personal honesty. People often have a sense of mythology about what is happening in their lives, built on a flawed understanding of reality. Collins calls this the "Stockdale Paradox" after the experiences of Admiral James Stockdale, a prisoner of war during the Vietnam conflict. Stockdale was tortured repeatedly yet held on when many others did not. When asked by Collins what the secret of his survival was, Stockdale said he had realistic expectations but never lost faith that he would get out. Stockdale said those who didn't endure were the optimists who thought they would be released soon. They lacked a sense of candor, of an honest assessment of their situation.

"This is a very important lesson," Adm. Stockdale told Mr. Collins. "You must never confuse faith that you will prevail in the end—which you can never afford to lose—with the discipline to confront the most brutal facts of your current reality, whatever they might be."[49]

Without regular, candid self-assessments, you could miss the full picture and foster self-deception. This will make you more apt to make mistakes, misjudge circumstances, and fail to weather storms of crises. Additionally, you could miss out on the fullness that knowing and trusting yourself brings.

## Overcoming Your Blind Spots

Larry King used to say, "I never learned anything while I was talking." Not only does active listening show respect for others and teach us about their concerns and interests, it can also lead to key insights about ourselves. Candid friends will shed light on our blind spots and tell us things we need to hear. However, these types of critiques are often given gently and may be missed entirely if we aren't paying attention.

So, what is a blind spot? If you have a driver's license, you *should* know what a blind spot is. It's that place where a car that is slightly behind but nearly beside you disappears from your mirrors. We, as drivers, know this blind spot could lead to a devastating accident if we didn't take steps to see past it. (This is why we glance over our shoulder before changing lanes.)

Blind spots occur in other areas of life as well. We can develop them in our thinking or emotions. They may not cause physical crashes, but they can lead to unintended consequences that hurt relationships and break trust. If we are aware that these kinds of blind spots exist, we will know to look for ways to see past them.

One tool to help us address our blind spots is the Johari window. This simple instrument demonstrates how other people can see our blind spots when we cannot. Created in the 1950s by psychologists Joseph Luft (Jo) and Harrington Ingham (Hari), the model shows we have things we know about ourselves and things we do not know. Equally important, we have things others know about us and things others do not know. When you align these two ideas, our blind spots are those traits that others see in us that we may not see in ourselves. Characteristics we don't see are likely our blind spots—weaknesses that could lead to loss of trust in our relationships.

Take a look at figure 6.3 of the Johari window and note the location of the quadrant known as the blind spot. This is the place where others know us better than we know ourselves. This spot offers an opportunity for learning and growth.

|  | KNOWN TO SELF | NOT KNOWN TO SELF |
|---|---|---|
| KNOWN TO OTHERS | ARENA | BLIND SPOT |
| NOT KNOWN TO OTHERS | FACADE | UNKNOWN |

*Figure 6.3*

So, how can you reduce your blind spots? We all need people who will be honest with us, especially about their observations of our behaviors. Surround yourself with people who will tell you the truth with love or respect—someone who will be candid with you. Then have the grace and humility to accept their insights without defensiveness, but with the determination to improve. Decide to navigate your relationships as safely and skillfully as you do your car—adjusting for blind spots along the way.

I (Omayra) have learned that I have to be proactive in ensuring there are people around me who understand the vital role they play in helping me recognize my blind spots. While so often we would like to believe that everyone is comfortable playing this role, experience has demonstrated that in reality we must often and repeatedly encourage others to share this necessary information.

## 5. Commit to Forgiveness

When you have a culture of candor, there must be a commitment to the idea of forgiveness. Forgiveness is the physical, emotional, and mental freedom to let go of mistakes, misdeeds, and mistrust. This does not mean you are to be naïve or trusting of those who do not deserve it, but you cannot let their actions inhibit you from moving forward.

This may be the most powerful example of your character to others. When you exhibit the ability to work through the misdeeds and wrongs set upon you, people will extend to you an added measure of respect. You will have the ability to earn trust where others cannot and grow relationships where you may not think it possible.

The other side of forgiveness is the importance of forgiving yourself. When you make a mistake, you must take time to forgive yourself and not let that mistake prevent you from moving forward. We can hold onto regrets, already forgotten by others and no longer a real factor in our ability to do things that will create an insurmountable wall around our capacity to grow and thrive. Take time to let go of those things and keep moving forward. (For a fascinating look into this topic, read *Forgive to Live*[50] by Dr. Dick Tibbits.)

Let's pause a moment and think about how this is currently playing out in our own lives. Is there something in your past that you have not forgiven yourself for? What is preventing you from doing so? How will granting yourself forgiveness and grace allow you to develop and model healthy relationships?

Now examine your relationships with others. Who do you need to forgive in order to move forward? How is that impacting your own development? Only when we consider how these ingredients come together and start addressing opportunities can we begin to create the strongest trust.

## Apologies—the Bridge Between Candor and Forgiveness

Despite our best efforts, we will make mistakes. They might be rooted in self-deception, arise from a blind spot, or be the result of some other form of poor decision-making. When we fail, and especially when someone is hurt as a result, we must use the primary tool for recovery of lost trust: apology. Apologizing sounds simple, yet it's sometimes so hard to do. At its most basic level, an apology is about trying to set right something that has gone wrong, and if possible, to repair the damage.

First, an apology needs to be timely and equal to the misdeed. If it is "too little, too late," it is of minimal value. An apology begins with humility and is activated through candor. For an apology to be authentic and effective, you must first be humble enough to admit you made a mistake, candid and sincere in your regret, and able to avoid self-justification.

What happens after the apology is up to you, but it is critical to recovering lost trust. A sincere apology offered in a timely way will usually be appreciated, but it won't fully heal a broken relationship. Only time and future actions can do that. Perhaps you can think of your increased self-awareness and determination to do better as the final and ongoing piece of your apology.

## 6. Transparency... the Sign of an Authentic Relationship

Transparency is the ultimate manifestation of an authentic relationship. Honesty, respect, open two-way communication, and the ability to admit wrongs are all characteristics of transparency. Transparency is also expressed in letting the other person ask questions, trusting them to make decisions, asking them for feedback, being open to what they have to say, and being approachable to those around you.

In healthcare, we rely on a culture of transparency. For the safety of patients and to minimize medical errors, every staff member must feel empowered to bring issues to the forefront with no fear of retaliation. We rely on each other to question orders whenever there is a need to do so, and to be open to feedback. When a critical patient is undergoing a resuscitation, the team leader is expected to ask the entire group of healthcare professionals present if they have any input. We need to know that someone is looking out for our blind spots and will make us aware of them. It is important to remember that truly authentic relationships will allow for this type of discussion. And in our case, it is critical to the safety and well-being of those we care for. It is paramount to maintain our Hippocratic Oath: *First, do no harm.*

Let's review the elements of authenticity and how they ultimately lead to transparency in relation to our healthcare example above. When we care for patients in an emergency, the members of our team must all have clarity of purpose in our roles. We need to be fully present and engaged every moment. We must demonstrate respect to each other and to the patient, working toward the common goal of saving a life even if there is disagreement. We should be candid with each other when information needs to be shared. And when we misstep, we must ask for and seek forgiveness if we have wronged a team member (or accept an apology if we have been the person wronged). These elements are all essential to the ability of our team to function at the highest level consistently every day for the well-being of our patients.

Think about your relationships . . . do you feel that you and others engage with complete transparency? If not, this lack of transparency will be detrimental to the establishment of transformational trust.

Acting with transparency and candor should not mean acting without concern for how information will be received. We need to demonstrate empathy for people. We must be consistent with our actions in this way and have open discussion with no concern for retaliation or repercussions. Transparency allows our thoughts and motives to be clear to others.

## Reflection

1. Who comes to mind when you think of "authenticity"? What about that person makes you think of them as authentic?
2. Have you given people permission to speak freely into your life? Have you ever been told you have a blind spot?
3. Do you avoid apologizing or take shortcuts that make your apologies less sincere?
4. Why do organizations often shy away from transparency? Are the risks of transparency worth the rewards?

# CHAPTER SEVEN

# BE DEPENDABLE:
## KEEP YOUR PROMISES AND COMMUNICATE CONSISTENTLY

*"You can have a big resume and talk a good game, but*
*success in life comes down to one word: performance.*
*People will judge you not by what you say, but what you do."*
~Bill Frederick

Early in my career, I (Roy) had the good fortune of meeting many of the political and business leaders in Orlando, Florida, while serving as student body president at the University of Central Florida (UCF). One of those key people was Orlando Mayor Bill Frederick. Mayor Frederick was one of my favorite business contacts, and he extended an invitation for me to meet with him at any time. As a business student, aspiring graduate, and possibly a future elected official (a goal I have long since given up), I couldn't wait to meet with the mayor. Mayor

Frederick had led a movement to build up the city, open new doors internationally, pioneer public-private partnerships, and carry the region to the national stage in many new and innovative ways.

Our meeting was everything I hoped for and more. Mayor Frederick shared stories and provided insights into his career and service to my hometown. One key observation in particular has guided much of my life and my career since. It was the quote we opened the chapter with, and it's worth repeating.

"Roy," Mayor Frederick said with a wide smile, "you can have a big resume and talk a good game, but **success in life comes down to one word: performance**. People will judge you not by what you say, but by what you do." There is a parallel statement attributed to Theodore Roosevelt that says, "People don't care how much you know until they know how much you care."

These words have stuck with me all of these years because they are so true. In fact, both statements exemplify the "experiential" side of trust and our capacity to earn trust over time with the work we do for and with others. Consistent, reliable performance reflects dependability.

## Transformational Trust Attribute: Dependable

Guiding Principle: Keep Your Promises and Communicate Consistently

Dependability, our third attribute, is anchored on the experience axis and is critical to establishing trust in both personal and professional relationships. Your dependability helps others trust that you will deliver on your promises, complete a job, and solve problems. It is fostered through consistent communication and is the best defense in crisis issues. Ask yourself these questions: What does being dependable look and feel like to me? Am I dependable in my relationships? Can others count on me to keep promises, complete the work I start, and follow through on my commitments? Do I communicate consistently with others I work with?

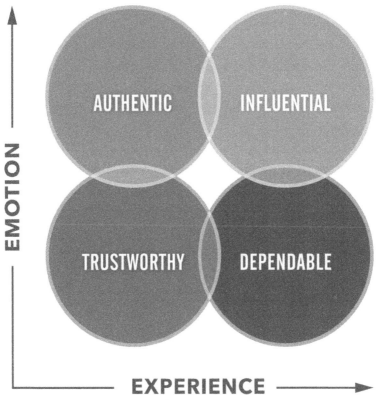

*Figure 7.1*

The more dependable you become, the more people will naturally learn to trust you. Dependability also encompasses the idea that you get the job done right . . . consistently. This consistency is seen in the execution of your responsibilities which reliably meet or exceed expectations.

In addition to doing good, consistent work, dependability also speaks to your ability to communicate effectively. Communication is a lubrication for getting things done and an elixir when things don't go well. An open architecture of communication with your family, friends, employees, and customers will—like a growing insurance policy for your reputation—help you to better manage expectations when problems arise.

All of us understand this on some level, but its importance cannot be understated. Let's take a look at another way to describe the same idea.

## Your Reputation Is Your Brand

Most of us have certain companies whose products or services we love to use. Typically, this is because the company makes excellent products or provides exceptional service or both. A company's brand is rooted in their reputation. It is the experience you expect to have when you use their product or service.

Dependability is foundational for your personal reputation and for a company's brand in the marketplace. Successful personal and professional brands are built on the fulfillment of promises made . . . one person, one experience at a time.

## Understanding a Brand Promise

Take a moment to think about a few of your favorite companies—the ones you return to again and again. What do you like about them? What makes them a "top brand" in your opinion?

One well-known company that effectively managed its reputation despite a potential crisis of trust was Johnson & Johnson. On September 29, 1982, three people died in the Chicago area after taking cyanide-laced Tylenol at the outset of a poisoning spree that would claim seven lives by the first of October. According to a report in *TIME* magazine, "Food and Drug Administration officials hypothesized that the killer bought [Johnson & Johnson's] Extra-Strength Tylenol capsules over the counter, injected cyanide into the red half of the capsules, resealed the bottles, and sneaked them back onto the shelves of drug and grocery stores.

"Without a suspect to revile, public outrage could have fallen squarely on Tylenol—the nation's leading painkiller, with a market share greater than the next four top painkillers combined—and its parent corporation, Johnson & Johnson. Instead, by quickly recalling all of its products from store shelves, a move that cost Johnson & Johnson more than $100 million, the company emerged as another victim of the crime and one that put customer safety above profit. Johnson & Johnson even issued national warnings urging the public not to take Tylenol and established a hotline for worried customers to call.

"Tylenol relatively quickly re-established its brand, recovering the entire market share it lost during the cyanide scare. Though things could have gone very differently, the episode's most lasting legacy has been in the annals of public relations, not poison control. The case has since become a model for effective corporate crisis management."[51]

Your experience with the companies you identified as top brands defines those relationships and determines the trust you have for them. Companies that you love are companies that give you a positive brand experience. Their reputation with you is strong. While brands can have a powerful effect on people and their purchase decisions, that relationship can turn sour with one bad experience. This is why companies work so hard to create good experiences with their products or services. Messing up in one of these areas can seriously damage their prospects for the future.

This is true in our personal relationships as well. The best-in-class brands are intentional about providing you with the best experience possible. And we should be as intentional as they are in building our brand. Of course, most of us don't use the word "brand" when we refer to the experience that other people have with us. Instead, we refer to it as our reputation. Whichever term we use, it is important to realize that the success of companies and individuals is built on trust, and trust is heavily influenced by a company's brand and a person's reputation.

## What We Can Learn from a Beloved Brand

When I (Omayra) was a teenager, I had a job at Disney World—one of the most beloved companies and biggest brands in the world. It was a fairly normal theme park job that many kids growing up in Orlando have experienced. However, that training turned out to be anything but typical in shaping how I saw people through the lens of my work. As part of the orientation experience, my new teammates and I were taught that we were "cast members"—not just employees. We learned that the company had certain expectations for how we were to act when we were "onstage" (i.e., in the park and interacting with guests) versus "offstage" (i.e., still on the job but not in areas where we interacted with guests). It was a fascinating way to think about work. To this day, I remember and occasionally employ some of the strategies and skills I learned as a Disney cast member.

If you've ever been to any of the theme parks, hotels, or attractions owned by The Walt Disney Company, you know you are not visiting an ordinary business. You enter a different world where nearly every conceivable detail has been considered and optimized. Adding to the entire experience, though, are the people who bring the adventure to life. When I worked for Disney, I felt as though the company empowered its employees to make a difference in a person's day. If a guest was having a poor experience, finding a way to make it better was not only within the scope of any employee's role but was expected. I believe this company-wide expectation helped preserve the Disney brand of service excellence.

Later in life, after I became a medical doctor, I saw an example of Disney's service excellence in action in a way I will never forget.

On a warm January morning in Central Florida, the day of the annual Disney Marathon, tens of thousands of runners and spectators from around the world thronged the route where the run would take place. The air was charged with excitement in anticipation of the event, the culmination of months and years of training for some athletes. As drove after drove of participants pressed to the starting line to begin the grueling 26.2-mile race, the crowd cheered their favorite runners.

One particular runner, Leith, started the race feeling great but began to have feelings of weakness as his run progressed. He wasn't worried, though. Leith had run many marathons in the past and was sure he just had to keep pushing himself to make it to the finish line. After crossing the finish line, however, he collapsed in front of his wife, who was waiting for him in the crowd. The onsite emergency medical team quickly cared for Leith and had him transported to a nearby hospital.

Meanwhile, Leith's son was still finishing his own run at the same marathon, completely unaware of what had happened to his father. When Disney cast members were informed of the situation, they sprang into action. As soon as they saw that his son had completed his race, they approached him and explained what had happened. They escorted him to where the rest of his family was anxiously waiting and personally took all of them to the hospital where Leith was being treated. Once Leith was stabilized and returned to good health, the same Disney cast members arranged to have the entire family return to Orlando to complete their vacation as previously planned.

This commitment to excellence—even amid difficult circumstances—made such an impression on me that it influences how I keep people's experiences with me, my team, and my emergency department top of mind. I do my best to educate my staff about being onstage versus offstage and empowering everyone on the team to step up and help when service recovery is necessary. While we should never lose sight of the importance of the lifesaving measures we provide, the manner in which they are delivered is also significant and becomes a key part of our brand.

## Make It Personal

Regardless of the setting or situation, all of us can strive to make every interaction with individuals important, recognizing that everything we say or do contributes to how dependable or undependable they see us in meeting their needs. That's what great brands and great people do.

One way to view the word "brand" is simply the idea of a promise delivered. For instance, when a company sells a product or service, we expect them to deliver on it. Our ensuing experience with them either reinforces our belief in that promise or destroys it. How many times have you walked away from a company because of a bad experience? How many times have you walked away from a relationship because of a bad experience? Trust or reputation can take a lifetime to build and can be lost in the aftermath of one bad decision.

Research shows that the experience a person has with a brand defines their perception of that brand's product or service. One international study found that a positive "brand experience"—the way a consumer experiences a brand's product or service—creates trust and loyalty with that brand for the future.[52]

Let's examine that concept from a personal perspective. Dependability is one of the main qualities that defines a strong brand. This same principle is at work in our personal and professional relationships. How others "experience" you influences what they believe about you. If they know you are dependable, they will tend to trust future interactions with you.

## Brand YOU

What is the state of your brand or reputation? Have you thought about it? Is it what you would like it to be? Consider the following lists of positive and negative descriptors. If you are being completely honest with yourself, which of these adjectives would you say others would use to describe you (this represents your current reputation)? Are they attributes you are proud of? How would you like to shift your brand? Which negative attributes would you like to eliminate, and which positive ones would you like to develop?

It's important to make time to consider these questions and take action to change if you aren't where you want to be. As Margaret J. Wheatley said, "Without reflection, we go blindly on our way, creating more unintended consequences, and failing to achieve anything useful."

## Positive Words

| | | |
|---|---|---|
| Accountable | Goal Oriented | Reasonable |
| Attentive | Grateful | Resourceful |
| Authentic | Great | Respectful |
| Available | Honest | Responsible |
| Bold | Humble | Reverent |
| Candid | Proactive | Righteous |
| Cheerful | Person Of Integrity | Sensitive |
| Committed | Joyful | Sincere |
| Confident | Kind | Strong |
| Consistent | Knowledgeable | Thankful |
| Courageous | Loyal | Thorough |
| Creative | Nurturing | Thoughtful |
| Decisive | Optimistic | Transparent |
| Dependendable | Orderly | Unstoppable |
| Determined | Original | Punctual |
| Diligent | Passionate | Purposeful |
| Disciplined | Patient | _____ |
| Enthusiastic | Peaceful | _____ |
| Fair | Persevering | _____ |
| Firm | Persuasive | |
| Flexible | Poised | |
| Generous | Prudent | |

## Negative Words

| | | |
|---|---|---|
| Agitated | Hesitating | Undependable |
| Aimless | Impatient | Unfair |
| Ambitiousness | Inattentive | Unfaithful |
| Apathetic | Indecisive | Unhappy |
| Biased | Indifferent | Unimaginative |
| Careless | Insensitive | Uninformed |
| Cowardly | Insincere | Uninspired |

| | | |
|---|---|---|
| Deceitful | Irresponsible | Unreasonable |
| Devious | Irreverent | Unresourceful |
| Discouraging | Lazy | Unstable |
| Dishonest | Nervous | Unsteadfast |
| Disloyal | Ordinary | Unsteady |
| Disorganized | Pessimistic | Unwise |
| Disrespectful | Powerless | Unthankful |
| Egotistical | Tardy | Weak |
| Fake | Timid | _____ |
| Fearful | Unaccommodating | _____ |
| Gloomy | Unaccountable | _____ |
| Greddy | Unappreciative | _____ |
| Harsh | Unavailable | _____ |
| Heeless | Unconvincing | _____ |

## The Competitive Advantage of Dependability

In chapter 5, we spoke of Roy's time with Consensus Communications. His position as partner was one of the defining roles of his career. The consulting firm specialized in high-stakes and crisis communications, and worked with major brands like Walmart, CSX, and Walt Disney Resorts. In addition, Consensus Communications provided general marketing and communication services to a broad number of businesses. The following story of one of Consensus's clients illustrates the importance of dependability and how it can be leveraged for a competitive advantage.

Consensus had been retained to develop a marketing program for a law firm. The firm, which operated throughout Florida, was celebrating its fiftieth year in business and recognized its need for a more proactive approach to marketing.

The first step Consensus took in the development process was an interview with the key attorneys in the firm to refresh their biographies, learn more about the firm's competitive position, and identify potential opportunities. It was quickly apparent that the attorneys had very good relationships with their clients, strong reputations, and little or no communication outside the specific work they were given. In many cases, an attorney would be working with a client on their particular transaction or litigation and delivering outstanding results, yet the client would have no awareness of the other areas of practice the firm offered. This was an opportunity for the firm to invest in the client relationships.

The team at Consensus developed a customized client cultivation program. The idea was simple: the attorney responsible for the client relationship would schedule a non-billable meeting with the key contact and the local managing partner (or the chairman of the firm if the opportunity was right) to discuss the client's satisfaction with the firm's work and service. A short questionnaire was sent out ahead of the meeting to provide some context and allow the client to clarify their thoughts. In addition, the attorneys would inquire about the challenges and issues the client was facing or anticipated. They would also spend time discussing other services the firm provided, should those services be needed.

Clients welcomed these visits. During the conversations, the firm learned much about what was going well and some about service concerns that could be improved upon. Most importantly, in 80 percent of the meetings, the attorneys came back to the office with new matters and work they would not have gotten otherwise.

Think about that for a minute. The firm invested only a few hours of time (perhaps a day or two if they had to fly somewhere) and a bit on travel expenses to spend non-billable time with a client to cultivate the relationship. The return on that investment was significant. First, they strengthened a loyal relationship with a valued customer. Second, they learned how they might improve that connection and compete on future work opportunities. And finally, they were handed new work just for showing up and caring about the client relationship. The firm was able to leverage its proven dependability to secure additional work outside its current scope.

How are you investing time to fortify your relationships? What additional benefits might result from those investments?

As we shared in the chapter about authenticity, there is nothing like presence to demonstrate how you care for someone and value them. Dependability is your strategic edge in life, like Mayor Frederick shared with Roy over lunch many years ago; performance makes a difference.

## Four Actions That Will Make You More Dependable

To achieve your desired personal brand, you must be seen by others as dependable for delivering on the promises made. While this is equally true in both personal and professional relationships, this concept is perhaps easiest illustrated through workplace interactions. For this reason, we'll discuss four actions that can create your "Strategic EDGE" in achieving dependability that is transformative. Once you see how these behaviors are applied in a professional setting, you can easily adapt them for use in your personal relationships. This is how to achieve a Strategic EDGE:

- **Engage**
- **Deliver**
- **Give**
- **Evaluate**

### 1. **Engage** Fully in Your Relationships and Your Work

People are important, and work is too. Sometimes when life gets busy, we focus on one or the other. But both are vital to long-term success.

If you focus more on people than on the quality of the work, for example, you may simply show up to work, "check the box," and do the bare minimum. This is a common practice for many. They merely comply with what they're told, complete their obligation, and believe that's all they need to do. But simply showing up is only sticking your toe in the water. Being engaged, on the other hand, is diving in and taking risks alongside everyone else. People around you can feel the difference. The quality of your work matters. To boost trust, be committed to engaging on the highest level and doing your best work.

If you focus more on the work to be done and care little, if at all, about the people involved, you'll miss the mark as well. The truth is relationships matter tremendously in every area of our lives. To succeed, we need to engage and cultivate our relationships in ways that build trust. This means being fully present, treating people like human beings (not like cogs in a wheel), and appreciating and respecting relationships. When you focus on performing high-quality work and building positive relationships, you boost the trust people have in you. For each of these concepts, we have provided some action steps for you to build your strategic edge.

So, how do you engage fully in relationships *and* work?

**ENGAGE ACTION STEPS:**
- **Be committed to quality** work, doing more than is expected of you. Your reputation rides on the results you deliver.
- Treat each person you work with as important, and **build strong relationships** with them.
- **Take your commitments seriously** because they can make or break your reputation.

## 2. **Deliver** Results on Time or Early

In order to deliver outstanding results, you must first clarify the expectations of your family member/friend/customer/client/boss. A simple conversation with them should reveal those unstated assumptions that could potentially be problematic. Once you clearly grasp the expectations, write them down. Show them to the other person (or your team) to make sure everyone agrees on them. Next, take time to lay out a process for how you will complete the steps to meet each one. If this is a group effort, actively engage your team in the process. Then you can practice accountability with yourself and your team.

Second, nailing down timelines is important. Make sure everyone involved agrees on the timeline and the specific deadlines involved. Review your progress regularly to be certain you're keeping up with your stated timeline. NOTE: There will be occasions when you miss the delivery or deadline. When that happens, make sure you have communicated *in advance* to the family member/friend/customer/client/boss (or whoever requested your services) and explain the reason for the delay and what you are doing to mitigate the problem. Don't wait until *after* you miss a deadline to communicate that a problem exists. This is how you manage expectations and ensure that damage to the relationship is minimized.

Communication is the functional tool that will help you better manage relationships and ensure that you are effectively delivering results. We'll unpack communication more in chapter ten. Just remember, good communication is a trust booster.

**DELIVER Action Steps:**

- Only **make commitments** you know **you can deliver on**.
- **Understand** the **expectations** of everyone involved.
- **Write down commitments, the steps** needed to complete them, **and** agreed-upon **deadlines**.
- If you run into delays, **communicate** them in advance of the deadline, not after you've missed it.
- **Do what you said you would do**. Deliver on time or early if you can.

## 3. **Give** People a Reliable Experience

Whether you are interacting with individuals or companies, they will want a reliable experience. Think of the most popular fast-food restaurants out there. One of the things they are known best for is consistency.

No matter if you order an item from their menu in Florida, Oregon, Maine, or California, your expectation is that it will be the same each and every time you buy it.

There's power in reliability, for companies and for you. But let's face it, most of us are not consistent in every area of life. We can all make improvements. Work on developing the habit of reliably delivering your best and even exceeding the expectations of others. Embed the steps you take to get there into your personal "standard operating procedure" to establish habits of excellence. Many of the characteristics we've discussed previously, including focus, attitude, perseverance, and integrity, all come into play here. If necessary, one idea is to engage a friend, coworker, or family member to help you practice your performance of consistency and perfect its delivery. Train yourself via establishing a consistent practice in order to boost trust.

In *Atomic Habits*, James Clear says, "Every action you take is a vote for the type of person you wish to become. No single instance will transform your beliefs, but as the votes build up, so does the evidence of your new identity."[53]

**GIVE ACTION STEPS:**
- **Stay focused on your purpose**. Remind yourself why a habit of consistency is important for long-term success.
- **Work on one area at a time**. Make that thing a habit before moving on to the next.
- **Practice reliability** with every interaction.
- **Don't overcommit**. Invariably, taking on too much will sabotage the reliability you're trying to achieve.

## 4. **Evaluate** Everything for Improvement

People walking away from an experience with you are evaluating it and determining if they want to come back for more. Everything that matters to us warrants evaluation. Hold yourself accountable to improve your performance. This, in turn, will help improve your relationships and boost trust.

One simple way to do this is to ask people for honest feedback on your performance and then listen without judgment to their response. Author Jack Canfield recommends a simple two-step evaluation approach. First, he says to ask people for feedback on your performance on a scale of 1 to 10. Second, if their response is anything less than a 10, ask what it would take to make it a 10.[54] Following are some example questions you could use for step one:

*On a scale of 1 to 10, how would you rate . . .*
- The quality of the work I just completed?
- Me as a boss?
- My listening skills?
- My response to the problem?
- Me as a spouse?
- How I conduct meetings?

Second, if the answer comes back as *anything less* than a 10, then you ask the follow-up question:

*What would it take to make it a 10?*

Don't get defensive or try to justify yourself or your performance. Simply listen, note what the other person says, and learn from their response so you can grow. Maybe you won't agree with their assessment of you, or perhaps you will. Either way, the feedback is valuable to understanding how others perceive you.

Be sure to ask for input on their whole experience as well: How was the overall quality of the product or service? How were your interactions with our team members? Evaluate every aspect of the experience to see what could be improved.

EVALUATE ACTION STEPS:
- **Request feedback** on your performance and the performance of your company/product/team.
- Find a way to **quantify performance** feedback, such as by using a numeric scale.
- If your customer found something suboptimal, **seek ways to improve** it.
- **Don't get defensive** or try to justify your performance. Simply use it to improve.

## A Credo for Dependability

I (Roy) am frequently telling people that when I grow up, I want to be Ben Hoyer. Ben began his professional life as the pastor of a small church in Orlando, Florida. Seeking to make a community impact beyond the doors of his church, Ben opened a coffee shop in downtown Orlando with an interesting business model: name your own price. That is, you pay only as much as you want for each cup of coffee. Working with independent, fair-trade growers from Guatemala, Ben utilized the proceeds to fund community projects. The company, Downtown CREDO, expanded to work with growers from Nicaragua in 2012, helping the farmers sustain their collective.

Over the years, CREDO has opened four locations in the Orlando area. Ben has also partnered with like-minded people and organizations to foster growth in the social entrepreneurial sector of Orlando. Examples of his collaborations include a funding/mentoring program called Rally Makers and CREDO Conduit, a coworking space in collaboration with Sungate Studios in Orlando.

What drives Ben is a clear purpose to serve others and the philosophy that his meaning must be bigger than himself. CREDO's name was inspired by the statement of belief Ben adopted:

*Life is worth living. I refuse to merely exist. I pursue a life of meaning and purpose, fulfillment and joy. The world is not yet as it ought to be. Neither is my city. Neither am I. Yet, I reject apathy and despair. I engage the world, my city, and myself to make an impact for good. I am not alone. I press through narcissism, isolation, and self-sufficiency, striving to live in authentic community.*[55]

In an interview on the blog *Outrageously Remarkable*, Ben tells how his vision followed his purpose. It inspired his ideas and set him on a path to transform his city. Along the way, Ben has leveraged his influence to show people how they too can help.

*I just started partnering with four local charities, went to them and said, "What are you not doing that you'd like to be doing?" and so I started organizing events. But I got into coffee because part of my credo says: "The world is not yet as it ought to be. Neither is my city. Neither am I. Yet, I reject apathy and despair. I engage the world, my city, and myself to make an impact for good."*[56] *So, I wanted to show people that there are global problems, but you will like yourself better when you realize you can impact them. You don't have to get apathetic and say that this problem is too big for me, there's nothing I can do to help it. I believed that coffee was one place where things aren't how they ought to be, and this guy I knew was already going down to Guatemala, so I just got on a plane and went down there, too.*[57]

Ben recognizes that you can transform your community by showing up every day committed to a credo, keeping your promises, and delivering a consistent and reliable experience. He has done this through the coffee shops, developing a strong brand for social entrepreneurship and partnering with other community influencers. He inspires people to make a difference in their areas of influence, by showing them how their acts of any size contribute to making the world a better place.

Ben followed the same path as others who have established a strong brand through dependability and trustworthiness. He exemplifies purposeful, meaning-driven action—fully engaging in work, delivering on promises, performing reliably, and continually evaluating his performance for opportunities to improve. This is what a strategic EDGE looks like.

## Reflection

1. Consider the steps in the strategic EDGE. How are you doing at engaging in your relationships? Are you delivering in the way you said you would?

2. Where have you given an exceptional experience? How did that contribute to the relationship?

3. When you have sought an evaluation from others, how did you receive the feedback? How did you use it to improve in the future?

*CHAPTER EIGHT*

# BE INFLUENTIAL:
# *BE A GOOD STEWARD OF YOUR TRUST*

*"The ultimate measure of a man is not where he stand
in moments of comfort and convenience, but where
he stands at times of challenge and controversy."*
~Martin Luther King Jr.

Ultimately, transformational trust is about using the influence we have—however great or small—to make a real difference in the lives of others. We can see this in the examples set by iconic leaders in history and on the world stage and in the small acts of kindness that people around us make each and every day. It begins with the intentionality we have in our relationships. Our contributions don't have to be world-changing, just meaningful to the people with whom we've been entrusted to serve and in those divine appointments that come our way.

Tim McKinney has led a varied career. He's been both a professional umpire and a real estate mortgage broker. But perhaps most interesting of all is his advocacy role for a Central Florida community called Bithlo. Over the years, Tim has built his level of influence throughout Orlando and used it to illicit help to transform Bithlo, one of Florida's poorest areas.

Bithlo had little in the way of infrastructure, transportation, or economic opportunity. Poverty rates were high, and a significant number of residents lived in mobile homes, many of which were dilapidated and moldy. An illegal garbage dump and a petroleum spill contaminated the community's well water, leaving it all but undrinkable. Illiteracy was common among Bithlo's estimated 8,200 residents, and with public bus service suspended because of budget cuts, locals had little hope that they could travel elsewhere for help.

Tim learned of these conditions when he became the primary caregiver to his aging great aunt. Over the course of time, he decided he must do something—anything—to help this community. So Tim founded United Global Outreach (UGO) to serve the residents of Bithlo and develop programs to meet their needs.

Tim began looking for the best way to help people transform their lives by gaining access to necessary services, finding employment, and improving the infrastructure and services of the town. He did this by earning the trust of others, building relationships, and leveraging his influence to make a difference.

When he started out, Tim didn't have a team of people to draw support and encouragement from. It was just him. But he wasn't willing to let the situation remain that way.

Tim became a voice for change, calling for the Orange County Commission to clean up decades of illegal dumping that had occurred in the community. He also raised concerns with local transportation authorities over access to walkable streets, bus services, and other basic services. As he began to push for improvements, Tim realized he could not do it alone. That's when I (Roy) met Tim. He impressed me with his commitment to serve and his desire to influence others for the good of this underserved community. I saw an opportunity to help him develop a number of relationships and provide him with pro bono communication services to help him get his message out.

The first thing I did was introduce Tim to people I knew at Florida Hospital (now AdventHealth) and invite them to participate in the community transformation. Bithlo's medical needs were acute. When residents got sick, they had to drive—or take an ambulance—to a hospital fifteen miles away in Orlando. Their town of 8,200 had no doctor's office or urgent care facility.

Later, when a new federally qualified health center opened in Bithlo, it received more than four thousand visits in its first year. Previously, those four thousand patients would have gone to an emergency room where they would have been provided expensive emergency care, not designed to address chronic issues in the way a primary caregiver can through a relationship, treatment plan, and ongoing monitoring.

The health center, accompanied by dental and mental health services, is a product of the Bithlo Transformation Effort, now backed by dozens of partners, including AdventHealth. The collaboration between public and private partners focuses on ten areas necessary for overall wellness: education, transportation, housing, basic needs, a sense of community, healthcare, the environment, economic opportunity, arts, and athletics.

Since its inception, Tim's effort has resulted in sixty-five community organizations collaborating to bring a bus service, primary care, eye and dental care, mental health counseling, and a new private school to Bithlo. In addition, plans have been made for major road and infrastructure improvements, which will allow for water and sewer service in the most vulnerable neighborhoods. In a new town center called Transformation Village, a well provides access to clean, free drinking water. Finally, a neighborhood of affordable small houses, called Dignity Village, is slated to replace a rundown trailer park.

When interviewed by *Orlando Magazine* about his journey, Tim stated, "The experience with my great aunt made me realize there are people out there who can't defend themselves . . . I can't stand injustice. And to me, a great injustice has been done to these people [in Bithlo]. People out here are struggling to make it through 24-hour segments of their lives."[58]

When he began, Tim could never have foreseen the eventual impact of his work. Not only has the Bithlo transformation effort changed the lives of countless residents, it's also received a Roadmaps to Health Action Award from the Robert Wood Johnson Foundation as well as a NOVA Award from the American Hospital Association. Today, the ongoing Bithlo transformation effort is supported by private and public funds.

Though Tim didn't have much to start with, he didn't let that stop him from trying to do something where he saw a need. Over time, others came on board to help. In that process, Tim perfectly described the concept of influence:

"It's very important that everybody who joins this collaboration not come with their own agenda as the end result," he said. "Everybody, including the government, academic partners, business partners, and volunteers are all focused on the end result—which is very simply seeing Bithlo transformed into a community that we'd all want to live in."[59]

## Lessons from the Journey

Tim's story exemplifies how one person can make a difference and how anyone can be a good steward of their influence. Through good stewardship of trust and influence, you too can bring the right people together to change the world for the better. Ahead, we will examine influence more closely and learn five critical steps for cultivating it. For now, think about these lessons we can draw from Tim's example:

- Seek ways to **do good** with no expectation of return.
- Know **every effort counts**—no matter how small.
- **Ask for help**. Your greatest impact may be getting people with the right competencies in to assist.
- **Be courageous and embrace the challenge**. Most things worth doing aren't easy. Keep going.

## Transformational Trust Attribute: Influential

Guiding Principle: Be a Good Steward of Your Trust

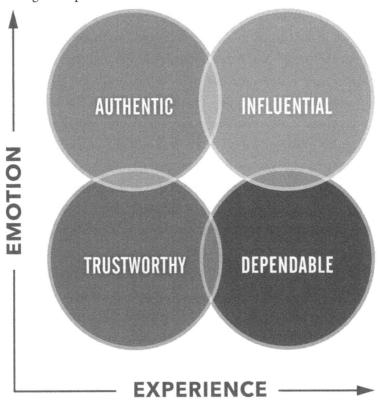

*Figure 8.1*

Influence is achieved as a result of the presence of the first three attributes. It's positioned at the pinnacle of both the emotional and experiential axes and is evident when we exercise the power of trust in a positive way for the people around us. Being influential requires the highest level of stewardship to make a difference in the lives of others. In fact, being a person of influence (however small or great) is often best accomplished by seeking whom we can help rather than focusing on our own wants and needs. In addition, the guiding principle of stewardship requires that we are equally intentional with whom we share our trust with and how they influence us.

## Use Your Influence to Help Others

Influence is the trust that changes lives, and the trademark of significant people throughout history. Influence is your ability to make a difference. People of influence have a much higher level of responsibility and accountability for the trust they have earned. "When someone has been given much, much will be required in return; and when someone has been entrusted with much, even more will be required."[60] People of influence exemplify the transformative level of trust to which we aspire.

Let's pause here and consider what this definition means. Some people would argue that they are not influential and do not desire to be. If that is you, we would like you to reconsider. We all influence others whether we realize it or not. Our influence may be positive (like when we use our time and talents to be of service to others) or our influence may be negative (like when we use other people only to get what we want for ourselves or encourage bad behavior). A positive influence comes from doing good for others, and a negative influence comes from being completely self-absorbed. This means we must be intentional in how we use our influence.

Research shows that people who are deemed trustworthy and have earned the trust of others have more influence. In the study "Trustworthiness, Trust and Influence in Organizational Decision Making,"[61] the authors wanted to find out whether the influence of employee representatives (eRs) increased within the organization when the eRs were considered trustworthy and trusted. They collected data from over six hundred HR managers across eleven European countries. The results showed a significant relationship between trustworthiness and the influence of eRs in decision-making within organizations. In other words, those who were perceived as more trustworthy had a greater influence within the company and were able to contribute to decision-making processes. The study presents "a unique view of the effects of trustworthiness and trust on the capacity to influence organizational issues." You can also be influential within your sphere by being trustworthy and building trust.

## Five Critical Steps in Cultivating Influence

Influence is a distinct attribute of leadership.

Martin Luther King Jr., Mother Teresa, Nelson Mandela, and Gandhi are names that are instantly recognizable. These were people of great influence whose actions made a tremendous impact on the people they served. Influential people such as these follow a consistent set of ideas and behaviors that we should model if we too wish to make a positive, significant impact in the lives of others.

### 1. Make the **CHOICE** to engage (and be decisive when saying "yes" or "no").

Influential people understand that choice is the most powerful tool we have, and they exercise it well. Every day we are confronted with choices in our life. Our decisions define us and how we are seen by others. From the small choices that may be a test of our integrity to the public involvement with a movement or controversial issue, none of our choices are insignificant.

### 2. Form **COMMITMENTS** openly.

Decisions require a full commitment to ensure they are carried out. People of influence step up and show others the importance of making commitments publicly or physically to create a sense of accountability for their choices.

Think about the people around you who inspire you and how they use this concept to move people to a new level of performance or improvement. This is the idea of "walking the talk" and is the outward manifestation of the choices we make.

Some examples of walking the talk are:

- A friend who says he wants to get healthier and shows up to work out each morning
- A minister who leads a mission trip after encouraging her congregation to serve more
- A president of a professional association who publicly announces she is taking the accreditation test to encourage others in her profession to follow suit
- A manager who shows up early to demonstrate the need to address an issue

### 3. Make better decisions through **CONFRONTATION** of issues—the good, the bad, and the ugly.

Critical to being able to ask all the right questions is the concept of humility, which was the first principle we learned in this program. Influential people exercise humility when confronting the issues, as they know deep down that they certainly don't know everything and need others to speak into the process. With the right authentic relationships, we can examine the issues facing us in achieving what we set out to do. Honest assessment is essential to knowing how best to exercise our influence.

### 4. Seek the **COMPETENCE** necessary to succeed and grow.

Once you have made the right choice, committed to your decision, and confronted the issues, you need to understand the scope of the work and develop the competence to do it. This can mean finding people to fill that role or perhaps taking time to learn the skills you need to do the job. Either way, influential people make the investment in the right people to do the right job.

### 5. Have the **COURAGE** to take on and finish the work.

Perhaps the most important quality of influential people is courage, recognizing the difficulties and challenges of something and still stepping up to take it on . . . and finish the work. Completing anything of significance will be difficult and requires all five of these qualities, but courage provides the push to move through the greatest challenges. Sometimes starting something is easier than seeing it through to completion. But don't give up. Some work may take a long time to finish, perhaps even a lifetime.

## Courage to Take on Giants

The well-known tale of David and Goliath tells of a simple shepherd boy who took on a giant soldier with no more than a sling, five smooth stones, and an abundance of faith. This story presents an overwhelming set of odds overcome by one person who would go on to lead a nation, consistently relying on his faith to overcome what were, from all outward appearances, insurmountable challenges. Bennet Omalu has just such a story.

Born in Nnokwa, Idemili South, Anambra, in southeastern Nigeria, Bennet no doubt never imagined he would become a modern-day "David" battling a modern-day "Goliath," the National Football League (NFL). Like David, he would credit his faith for giving him the strength and opportunity to go to battle on behalf of others.

Bennet's father, a man who had pulled himself out of poverty to become an engineer and a respected member of his community, insisted that all seven of his children get an education and accomplish great things. He always told his children that they were put on this planet to make a difference in the world. But Bennet was unsure of himself, quiet, and reserved. His father suggested that he become a doctor, so at age fifteen Bennet entered medical school.

All through school, he struggled. Bennet experienced an intense depression that his family was sure would lift after he graduated. But it didn't. After graduation, he applied for and received an invitation to become a visiting scholar in the United States. Bennet thought that, finally, his dreams would come true, and he would be happy. But in the US, things were confusing to him. With his accent, he wasn't always understood. He also encountered some who assumed he was uneducated because of the color of his skin. He cried out to God in discouragement. He wondered about his purpose and why he'd ever become a doctor.

One day the phone rang. The professor of pathology at the other end of the line extended an invitation to Bennet to become a pathology resident at Columbia University's Harlem Hospital Center. It was there during his first autopsy of a man who had died from AIDS that Bennet found fulfillment. He was finally doing something that he believed made a difference. Over the following months, he began to realize his purpose in his career as a medical examiner.

Years later, Dr. Omalu was serving as a pathologist for the city of Pittsburgh when he was brought the body of former Pittsburgh Steelers Hall of Fame player Mike Webster, who had been found dead at the age of fifty. Webster, fallen from the public eye, had been living in his car, depressed, addicted, and suffering from other mental illnesses.

In the autopsy, Dr. Omalu began to unravel a mystery that led him to a clear understanding of what had caused Webster's mental health problems and, ultimately, his death. The diagnosis was a kind of brain damage called chronic traumatic encephalopathy (CTE) caused by repeated blows to the head, previously discovered in autopsies of boxers. As time went on, Dr. Omalu and team had similar findings in autopsies of other former professional football players. Omalu, along with two colleagues from the University of Pittsburgh Department of Pathology, published their findings in the journal *Neurosurgery* in a paper entitled "Chronic Traumatic Encephalopathy in a National Football League Player." In the report, Omalu and his colleagues stated: "We herein report the first documented case of long-term neurodegenerative changes in a retired professional NFL player consistent with chronic traumatic encephalopathy (CTE). This case draws attention to a disease that remains inadequately studied in the cohort of professional football players, with unknown true prevalence rates."[62]

Omalu's work would set off a firestorm of debate regarding the safety of football in America and the NFL's responsibility for the recurring CTE and untimely deaths of former players. The issues would rage on for nearly a decade and would finally result in numerous safety changes to football and a major lawsuit involving more than five thousand former NFL players and the league. Dr. Omalu, once unsure of himself as a youngster, now testified before Congress about his findings. The story of his study of CTE and the opposition by the NFL was documented in the magazine *GQ* and later expanded into a book, *Concussion*. It was adapted into a movie by the same name.

Dr. Omalu is quick to say that his faith was a critical part of his ability to withstand the scrutiny of his work and the threats that ensued as he tried to bring the information he uncovered into the public arena and lobby for changes to protect players. In an article he penned for *Guideposts*,[63] Dr. Omalu shares the story of how his faith in God moved him to achieve his medical education, to persevere through many personal challenges including depression, and finally, to put him in a position to become the necessary voice of change for football players and their families. In the article, he concludes, "In my life, the light that led me from depression was the light of God, who has guided me in the darkest of times and the best."

Dr. Bennet Omalu's faith and his trust that God was guiding him even through some of the most trying moments of his life sustained him and gave him strength. It also helped him find his purpose, which gave his life significance and meaning. In his story, we see how faith, the highest expression of trust, provides an assurance that transcends the moments of doubt, frustration, despair, and anxiety that come with the challenges we all face in life.

You may not be called to be a voice in the public square as Dr. Omalu was; however, you are called upon daily to make a difference where you live and work, and faith can be a strong foundation to ensure you are prepared to do so. Your story, like that of Dr. Bennet Omalu, will be defined by how you come through struggle, how you engage and treat others, and what you have decided to live for.

## Who Deserves *Your* Trust?

So far we have focused on ways you can build transformational trust into all your relationships. As we've learned, trust is a gift that we should care for with our choices and actions. We must never squander it or take it for granted. In our own life, we must consider how we will share the gift of trust with others. Who deserves your trust?

Did you know that those whom you trust are, in some ways, a public reflection of you, your values, and your beliefs? In fact, many people will judge you based on the actions of those you associate with. Perhaps you've heard the expression "guilty by association"? It means the people you interact with can either enhance or damage your reputation and the trust people have in you. Parents know this to be true, which is why they warn their children about hanging out with untrustworthy people. An ancient proverb says:

*Do not be misled: bad company corrupts good character.*[64]

It's important to be mindful when you extend your trust to others. You must hold them accountable to the same standards to which you adhere. Since the reputation of those you trust reflects on you, trust only people who have earned it.

The four attributes of transformational trust provide the foundation that serves as a map for you to achieve deep abiding trust in your relationships and a set of standards by which to hold others accountable.

As you earn trust with others, they must also earn *your* trust. This is not to say you must approach relationships with an unwillingness to trust. You will often need to extend trust to others with whom you have little or no experience. However, you must keep your standards and expectations for their behavior high. You have a responsibility for resources and people who may be adversely affected by someone who does not prove to be trustworthy. A difficult lesson is that many people you meet and work with may not be deserving of your trust. In some unfortunate cases, they may even be the people you work for.

## "Bad Company"

The emergency department is a unique environment where trust is essential to the team's ability to provide excellent patient care in uncertain circumstances. A couple years ago, the ED where I (Omayra) work had several changes in the leadership structure. The new leaders, Susan and George, did not have the support of the staff. This was understandable because not only were they poor leaders, they were toxic.

Susan and George did not seek to earn the trust of the staff and instead consistently demonstrated behavior that alienated people and lost their trust. They were inconsistent in their communication and occasionally lied to the team. They sought to create a divide between the nursing staff and physicians. As time passed, the overall morale of the staff dropped disappointingly. The team collaborated less. Territorialism increased. Poor communication was rampant between leadership, clinical support staff, nurses, and physicians. A general level of distrust rose among everyone. Because of the increasingly toxic environment, patient satisfaction scores and clinical outcomes plummeted, and many excellent nurses and staff left the department.

After one year of poor results, Susan and George were removed from their roles. New leaders Barbara and Fred were placed in charge. Both had previously worked as nurses in the department. Each had already established themselves as well-rounded, trustworthy individuals and reliable colleagues. Recognizing the need to build and restore trust to help the emergency department succeed, Barbara and Fred decided to make an intentional effort to improve the level of trust in the department, knowing that doing so would probably fix most of the other issues present.

Fred and Barbara decided to engage the team by approaching this difficult situation with humility and vulnerability. They began by focusing on being personally reliable, consistent, and available. They specifically targeted increasing communications with all department staff, especially the clinical support staff, nurses, and physicians. Where previous leadership had consistently held back information from staff, the new leadership team chose to be transparent and accountable.

Barbara and Fred let it be known that all team members were to be treated with respect and dignity. They used positive reinforcement and constantly requested feedback, using it to better define performance improvement measures. Staff members began to feel appreciated and respected. As a result, our department quickly saw an improvement in clinical outcomes and patient experience. We also saw improved nursing retention and a desire from other departments to want to work with us.

What so recently was a dire situation now is a pleasant place to work because leaders set out to build a work environment based on trust.

## Toxic Leadership

Have you ever worked in a place where there is toxic leadership? Generally speaking, toxic leaders lack character as well as strong moral and ethical standards. Such leaders often appear to act out of selfish rather than selfless motives. They are more concerned with personal success rather than the success of the company or their team members. They often lack empathy for others. They frequently withhold information because knowledge brings empowerment, and the only ones they truly want to empower are themselves. Toxic leaders inspire no one and create a miserable work environment.

While no leader is perfect, every leader *can* be trustworthy by following the principles for building trust. What would happen in your company if everyone focused on trust-building behaviors? Not just the leaders, but everyone?

This type of leadership fosters a sense of safety, where people feel free to speak up, speak truth to power, and address issues of concern openly and without retribution.

Let's apply this personally. How many trust-building behaviors do *you* practice? Whether you are a leader or not, how do you engage others? What filter do you start with? Do you hold yourself accountable to the goals and mission of your company or team? Do you conduct yourself with humility and vulnerability?

In my work as a consultant, I (Roy) had the tremendous blessing of working with many trustworthy organizations. However, I also found myself in situations where clients and others proved to be otherwise. In those cases, I removed myself from a direct relationship—resigned the account, dismissed the contractor, or fired the employee—before that connection tainted the perception of my trustworthiness and that of my organization.

Untrustworthy relationships are toxic because they negatively affect all the other relationships in your life.

Influence is a powerful gift, given to us by others as an ultimate reflection of the trust they have in us. The work of a trust transformation is ongoing and requires that we remain mindful of each attribute, striving to grow in ourselves and cultivate each relationship. That said, each attribute builds on and feeds the others. Let's summarize how that occurs:

- **Trustworthy** – You trust yourself and have earned the opportunity to be trusted by others; people want to engage with you and extend to you the benefit of the doubt when problems arise.
- **Authentic** – Others view you as real, and you exhibit qualities such that people extend their trust and connect with you; you foster confidence in your relationships.
- **Dependable** – People now rely on you to fulfill identified roles or services; you manage relationships well with individuals, groups of people, organizations, and even communities.
- **Influential** – You seek the good of others, not just yourself; people may ask for your guidance, support, or leadership; you have honest, meaningful engagements and can bring people along with you in support of an idea/goal/vision.

## Reflection

Think back to a time when you had to break off a relationship with an individual or group of people that was untrustworthy.

1. What were the signs that the relationship was irreconcilable?
2. How did it adversely affect your health . . . your work . . . your thoughts?
3. What was the breaking point for you?

4. Did you know long before you took action that the relationship was adversely affecting your life?
5. Did any of your close friends, advisers, or family share concerns?
6. What good things happened (to your health, work, other relationships) once you were free from that relationship?

# CHAPTER NINE

# THE IMPORTANCE OF COMMUNICATION

*"Any fool can know. The point is to understand."*
~Albert Einstein

I t was another busy day in the emergency department where I (Omayra) work. An elderly male patient complaining of chest pain was rushed in via ambulance, accompanied by his wife, who was understandably quite concerned. Upon his arrival, an electrocardiogram was ordered to check his heart; the attending emergency medicine physician quickly identified the cause of his chest pain—a massive heart attack.

Within moments, an overhead page went out, a team mobilized, and the situation became an "all hands-on deck" type of incident. The emergency physician contacted the interventional cardiologist, and together they agreed the patient would benefit from immediate evaluation and possible intervention in the catheterization "cath" lab.

With the decision made, the emergency physician, multiple nurses, paramedics, and respiratory therapists prepped the patient for the cath lab. There, the procedure went like clockwork with everyone performing their best. Opening the clotted artery in time, our team saved the patient's life. His gradual recovery was smooth and uneventful.

The ED staff felt elated. Everyone had labored intensely and given their all, and their efforts had proven successful. They had achieved an optimal result for our patient in record time.

Needless to say, everyone expressed surprise when a few weeks later they learned the patient's wife had filed a complaint about the care she and her husband had received. Why? The wife complained that no one took the time to communicate with her while she was in the emergency department with her husband. No one told her what was going on and why. Rather than celebrating the outcome, the staff was left wondering what had happened. Who should have spoken to the wife? How had this step been overlooked?

## Communication Is Critical in a Crisis

When it comes to trust, the importance of good communication cannot be overstated. In fact, during times of uncertainty or great stress, communication becomes paramount. One might even say that during a crisis, overcommunication is not possible because people naturally want to know all they can; otherwise, their minds go to the worst-case scenario and fear sets in.

The two Chinese symbols that express the term "crisis" are "disaster" and "opportunity," which capture the crossroads that a crisis presents. In many ways, our response can dictate the outcome.

Have you ever had an interaction where you walked away and thought, *Wow, that went great!* but then later learned how poorly others thought it went? In healthcare, we have seen multiple examples where we thought we had done everything right with a patient, only to learn later of an area where we missed the mark—as illustrated in the above story.

After many years in healthcare, I can tell you communication is essential to creating the best patient outcomes. In addition, countless studies have demonstrated that physicians who communicate well are the least likely to be sued.[65] Communication provides the foundation of the transformational power of trust; when people are engaged and informed, they feel valued.

As with Roy's bracelet story in chapter 1, we often take for granted that a missed moment of communication can have a devastating result on our relationships. Earning and maintaining trust means being constantly aware of how our actions or inactions affect how we are perceived. The key point here is that we have to take responsibility for the relationships in our lives—both personal and professional. We must be mindful and intentional of trust.

## The Communication Challenge

A significant element in building trust is how well we communicate with others. Communication can often be complicated.

In *Leadership in the Crucible of Work*, Dr. Sandy Shugart says, "The most dangerous thing about communication is the illusion that it has occurred." Business expert Peter Drucker expands on this idea, "The most important thing in communication is to hear what isn't being said."[66]

## The UGLI Orange Exercise[67]

Have you ever heard of The UGLI Orange Exercise? It's a role-play that teaches about communication and conflict resolution.

Two people are sent to acquire an UGLI fruit (a cross between a mandarin orange and a grapefruit). This particular citrus fruit is available only once a year, and this season there is only one for sale. Each buyer is a scientist who needs a specific part of the fruit to solve a worldwide disaster. Here is the catch: the scientists work for competing companies—sworn enemies caught up in lawsuits and corporate espionage. To say the companies have no trust in each other is an understatement. The last thing each buyer was told by their bosses was, "Don't trust the other scientist."

This dilemma is a classic management training exercise commonly used in teaching negotiation or problem-solving skills. People are assigned one of the scientist roles and paired with the other scientist to see how they can each get what they need. As they are briefed, the distractions and issues regarding the company politics, current events, and world crises completely hide the fact that one of them needs only the juice and the other only the rind of the UGLI fruit.

As they talk, argue, and reread the case over and over, eventually real communication happens, and the light goes on. Once they clearly understand each other and see their needs are not conflicting, the scientists can not only solve the big problem (get the part of the fruit they require), but they can do it for half the price, if they team up with their rival to purchase the UGLI fruit together.

Clarity grows out of good communication. Clarity is essential to trust and to the first principle of authenticity. Once each scientist's purpose is understood (i.e. what part of the orange is actually needed) and communicated, a mutually beneficial outcome—even between rivals—can develop. People who possess clarity are far more efficient and effective in their work, and generally make better decisions than those without it.

Consider these other positive and negative aspects of communication:

## Some Positive Aspects of Communication

- Communication is powerful and necessary in building trust.
- Good communication opens doors.
- Communication provides assurance and contributes to a sense of safety.
- Communication connects you when the other person understands what's important to you.
- Communication is an ongoing process that we can improve every day.
- Communication is one of the best tools for recovering from broken trust.

## Some Negative Aspects of Communication

- Communication doesn't always happen, even when we think it has.
- Communication may be intended as positive but can still feel negative to the recipient.
- People sometimes hear what they want to hear, which may be quite different from what you are trying to say.
- Poor communication can quickly damage relationships.

Communication changes people, impacting what they know about us and how they understand our organization. Communication is the lifeblood that flows through relationships, informing and strengthening—at a micro level in our personal relationships and at a macro level in and out of organizations. Effective communication can go a long way to help grow, maintain, and protect your interests, while poor communication can feed disastrous results. Communication is a two-way process whereby we must work to understand all of the information shared with us in whatever form it is shared.

## Ways to Improve Communication

Some of us are naturally gifted communicators, and some of us are not. Those who aren't talented in this area are tempted to avoid it. But a lack of communication all too easily leads to a lack of trust. So let's discuss a few methods for building your communication skills.

- **Become a Good Listener** – By actively listening before you speak, you allow others to feel heard, and you get the chance to collect as much information and insight as possible.
- **Ask Clarifying Questions** – After someone speaks to you, try restating or mirroring what they said. Then ask clarifying questions to be sure you heard correctly. Confirm with them that your

understanding is accurate. Examples of this include repeating back their words and paraphrasing to confirm comprehension.

- **Notice Nonverbal Communication** – A person's body language sometimes communicates more clearly than the words they speak. Pay attention to eye contact and hand gestures to get a more complete picture of a person's feelings.

- **Be Clear and Concise** – Avoid the trap of believing people will understand better if you use more words to explain. Often the opposite is true. Keep your message short and sweet.

- **Be Honest** – In order for people to trust you, they need to know that you are being honest in your communication.

- **Show Empathy** – Good communication is difficult if you are only willing to see your own point of view. For this reason, be quick to empathize with other people's thoughts and experiences. The more you can see the world through their eyes, the more opportunities you will have to connect with them.

- **Focus on the Positive** – While differences of opinion or negative circumstances are easy to dwell on, try to find the common ground between you and stay focused on positive solutions. Don't avoid problems that need to be fixed, but move toward solutions you can agree on.

## Communicate with Stories

Most people love a good story. Stories are powerful and are often persuasive. They don't have to be long, but they should be interesting. If you are trying to communicate a point, consider using a story for illustration—especially if it would work better than cold, hard facts.

Remember, every person and organization has a story. Taking ownership of your story and telling it well is important. Because if you don't tell your story, someone else will. And they may not have your best interests in mind when they do. Ask yourself: *What do people know about me or my company? What do I want them to know?* In the following case, a lot of communication and positive action were required to overwrite the negative story that one particular physician had believed of my organization for so long.

## Overwriting a Bad Story

When I first met Dr. Bill Johnson, I sensed I was in trouble. He approached after I had just finished delivering a speech to the local Kiwanis Club about the new hospital that was going to be built in the community.

"Roy, I appreciate you coming here to talk to us, but I do not trust what you are saying," he began. "And just so you know, those people you work for caused me to have a heart attack. So, I will never set foot inside your hospital even if you do build it."

At age twenty-seven, I stepped into what I thought was a plum position when I became the public relations manager for a new medical center in Central Florida. Here we were bringing a state-of-the-art hospital to a neighborhood that had never had its own facility. With nearly 100,000 people in the service area, I assumed the community had to be thrilled we were there and would welcome us with open arms. Unfortunately, that was only half the story.

You see, there had been a real battle over who would build and run this new facility, and the locals had taken sides . . . half on one side and half on the other. Though we'd "won" the battle, the part of the community that had campaigned for our competitor did not trust us.

One of those skeptical community members was Dr. Bill Johnson. Dr. Johnson was a retired physician who had advocated for our opponent. Though he didn't know much about us, he didn't like us and certainly felt he couldn't trust us. Once I understood this, his gruff greeting made more sense.

Dr. Johnson immediately became the benchmark for my success, and his attitude inspired in me a personal responsibility for this undertaking.

His words at our first meeting captured the beliefs of many people I encountered in those early days. In fact, many determinants put trust at risk in this endeavor, and our team had to own all of them.

Employees and physicians came to work at the new medical center from four or five different hospitals, various competitors, and many different cultures. My job was cut out for me. Putting aside predispositions about our contribution to the community, our team had to intentionally build trust from the inside out, seeking ways to engage in relationships that would earn and cultivate trust. What meant the most was that our CEO and leadership team was sold on the idea of building trust first.

We started by creating specific venues to build trust.

First, we formed a series of advisory boards and small community outreach groups. We recruited key stakeholders to serve on a general hospital advisory board, which would drive the organization of opening events and development of ideas for reaching other important constituents. We began a program targeting physician office managers, offering resources for running their offices and protocol development, as well as the opportunity to make connections with our people and other initiatives.

Next, we went out to groups of employees and physicians and conducted town hall–style meetings and other events where we could address their questions and concerns in an open, transparent fashion. The suggestions were taken back to leadership meetings, and many of the recommendations were accepted.

Finally, we launched a communication campaign designed to reflect our intention of building trust. We called the campaign "Hand in Hand" and focused on the importance of all the hands that brought healthcare to this community—those that built the hospital, delivered care, supported the hospital, and volunteered their time and talents.

In our communications, we sought participation from as many people as possible to celebrate the results of the many hands that made the hospital a reality. One of our efforts was to collect handprints from people throughout Florida to recognize everyone's contribution. To accomplish this goal, we sent out thousands of papers with a place where people could outline their hand and decorate it. The campaign was a huge success.

Though it happened gradually, the positive transformation of the community's perceptions of the hospital and their trust of us was evident at the opening night gala event. Standing at the entrance to the venue, I saw Dr. Johnson wearing a tuxedo and an enormous smile, serving as one of our hosts. The man who at one time had assured me he would never set foot in our medical center had now become one of our biggest supporters.

One final note of interest is that our hospital was on a plan to break even after three years. However, we beat that metric and began to operate in the black within eighteen months. Many elements determine a hospital's performance; however, the culture and connections that can be made in an environment where trust is put first are two vital, elevating factors.

## Reflection

1. Describe a time when you thought communication you provided was adequate but later learned it was unsuccessful. What lessons from above would have helped this be a more favorable outcome?

2. Do you use these same principles for good communication with your family and loved ones? If so, consider the benefits. If not, how can you begin to implement these each day?

# CHAPTER TEN

# HEALTHY CONNECTIONS

*"Trust is like blood pressure. It's silent, vital to good health,
and if abused it can be deadly."*
~Frank K Sonnenberg

There are fundamental parts of our lives that are intangible, like love, and are essential to our ability to thrive. Even though we can't necessarily hold these things and they are not physical objects, they are real, nonetheless. Qualities we ask for, like patience, can be manifested as behaviors and actions. Trust is one of these intangible yet necessary elements of a thriving life. Trustworthiness and a belief in integrity in ourselves can be reinforced in our own behaviors and actions.

In times of stress and challenge, it can be easy to have a multitude of excuses for not holding to the same steadfast commitment to integrity, positivity, consistency, authenticity, and responsible influence. We often have others in our lives who help us remain true to these values and hold us accountable. But what happens when you don't have these individuals around? How do you maintain these values?

During the COVID-19 pandemic, our lives were changed dramatically within days. Our social networks were impacted when we could no longer safely see each other face-to-face. Schools, businesses, gyms, and most other establishments closed. Many used these spaces and networks to hold themselves accountable. What would they do now?

I (Omayra) was fortunate that before the COVID pandemic spread in 2020, my husband, Fred, and I already had established a set of habits to help us maintain our physical and mental health—including a daily exercise routine. We awoke each weekday morning to work out together in our garage gym. We held each other accountable, and on days one of us felt too tired to get up, the other would provide the encouragement to do so. Both of us knew that this intentional focus on physical wellness had a significant positive impact on mental health, too. While so much was changing in the world at large, keeping this routine constant, practicing self-care, and holding each other accountable provided normalcy and a pressure release for us.

Staying true to my fundamental values and commitment to healthy behaviors helped me maintain my ability to trust myself during an unprecedented time. Even so, there were moments when the pressures of the day were so acute that I had to take drastic steps to reset my focus and reclaim my joy.

Early in the pandemic, there was one particularly difficult day while working at the hospital. We were already physically and emotionally exhausted when we received the news that patient counts were predicted to rise to a staggering number in the coming days. If true, the needed care would overwhelm the abilities of the hospital staff. As a leader, it was difficult to hear these statistics and realize that I had to appear unflustered and calmly lead my team through something I had never before seen.

Driving home that evening, I received a phone call from my best friend Brooke who called to see how I was doing. As I told Brooke about my day, I felt afraid and overwhelmed. In fact, I had a sense of despair at the thought of what was to come.

As I got closer to home where my two children and husband were waiting, I realized that I would not succeed at being a mom or wife if I went in the house with such gloom. I knew I had to reframe my thoughts, be intentional about thinking positively, and somehow find joy in the moment to counteract the sense of despair. After hanging up with Brooke, I went into the house, walked straight through the kitchen, and headed to the backyard. On the way, Fred asked me what I was doing. I told him I was jumping in the pool (fully clothed). I knew that this would be entirely unexpected for my children to see. In fact, they were surprised and gleeful. I decided to pull my daughter in with me. The joy and giggles that came after were exactly what I was hoping for . . . and what I needed.

If we don't maintain our self-care, we can't trust ourselves to perform at our highest levels. *Do you trust yourself enough to have and maintain a self-care system?* If we can't trust ourselves, we certainly can't expect others to trust us. There are everyday self-care behaviors we can adopt that can help us maintain our trustworthiness. Whether we practice habits that build physical health, mental clarity, or an outlook of joy and gratitude, our daily choices contribute to our journey of transformational trust.

## The Mind-Body Connection with Trust

Since our mind, body, and emotions are intimately connected, what happens to one can have a powerful influence on the others. It may seem surprising, but our physical habits can affect our mental and emotional health. If our emotions are all over the place and those around us don't know what to expect, they may have a hard time extending their trust to us. But demonstrating consistency by being "steady" mentally and emotionally will help others to see us as trustworthy.

Take a moment to think about the basic behaviors and habits that you maintain. Ask yourself the following questions and consider how often you are able to practice healthy choices:

- How much sleep do I get on a regular basis? Is it an adequate amount?
- Am I exercising regularly?
- How frequently do I assess the level of my stress and how am I managing it?
- Am I making time for myself?
- Am I able to connect with others frequently enough to feel fulfilled? What does my network of non-work friends look like?
- How am I nurturing myself through my food choices every day?

While we would like to believe that we are consistently achieving success in these areas, we often find aspects of self-care that we can improve. As we develop greater trustworthiness, or trust in ourselves, we must be more intentional and accountable for self-care. It's the most visible manifestation of trustworthiness. Let's review these fundamental behaviors, their importance in shaping our relationships and trust, and then consider a useful, habit-based approach that can help us enhance our current opportunities.

## The Sleep Connection

Sleep experts tell us we need seven to eight hours of sleep every night for optimal health, but many of us get much less than that. We believe we can cut our sleep short without it harming us. Sleep deprivation can not only affect us physically but can wreak havoc on us mentally and emotionally by causing increased irritability, impaired judgment, negative moods, anger, anxiety, and depression. Not the characteristics we're striving toward if we want to be more trustworthy. Work toward getting the recommended amount of sleep each night to help lift your mood and maintain a positive attitude. Drs. Rebecca Robbins and Manoucher Manoucheri, in *The REST of Your Life*, offer many strategies for getting a better night's sleep and thus improving your mental outlook. You will be amazed how this simple lifestyle change can make such a difference.

The first step to allowing yourself this time for sleep is to plan ahead and schedule seven to eight hours. Create a bedroom that is comfortable, cool, and dark. Don't use electronic devices at least thirty minutes before you turn in. Set your phone to a nighttime mode and silence it so its lights and sounds do not disturb your rest. Don't exercise or consume alcohol in the several hours preceding bedtime. Engage in an activity that will allow you to unwind before you plan on sleeping, like reading a book. Just as you may have a morning routine, create a regular nighttime routine that tells your body that you will soon rest. Getting sufficient sleep makes us more energized, productive, and focused, helping us build trust more easily. Your positive outlook is sure to enrich all your relationships.

## The Exercise Connection

Besides helping you lose weight and improve your overall health, exercise plays a powerful role in maintaining a positive outlook, boosting your self-esteem, and improving your sleep. More than that, it reduces stress and anxiety and helps fight depression. Researchers from University College London discovered a link between a lack of physical activity and high rates of depression.[68]

Exercise releases endorphins, which promote a general feeling of well-being. Experts recommend that adults get 150 minutes of moderate aerobic exercise every week. If you're not there yet, start out small and work up to the optimal amount. You don't have to do it all at once; simply incorporate more movement daily. Schedule time to exercise— just thirty minutes a day, five days a week.

I (Omayra) have found that the habit of preparing for exercise ahead of time improves the likelihood that I will follow through. My husband and I write out our planned workout the evening before, and make our workout shakes in advance. If you treat your time for exercise like you would any other scheduled commitment, and make a habit of doing so, you will find it is much easier to get it done. After even just one session, you will immediately start to feel the positive effects on your mental and emotional state. Your mind, body, and emotions will thank you, and you may discover trust is easier to build with the increased positivity you'll have.

## The Stress Connection

Another factor that can affect our interpersonal relationships and therefore the level of trust in our lives is stress. We all face stress. And that's not necessarily a bad thing. But as Drs. Dick Tibbits and Nick Hall point out in *The Stress Recovery Effect*, we need the right amount of stress—not too much so we become exhausted and overwhelmed, and not too little so we become bored and frustrated. The ideal amount of stress will enhance our creativity, performance, and satisfaction with life. Too much stress can precipitate a drop in serotonin, though, resulting in increased aggression, irritability, and depression. It's hard to be trusting or trustworthy when we're feeling like that. Stress can also increase your blood pressure and risk for heart disease, and weaken your immune system.

When you feel overwhelmed, don't dismiss your feelings of stress. Identify healthy strategies to help you handle stress when it gets to be too much. Discuss your stress level with your doctor to identify how it may be impacting your overall health. Learn what helps you best relieve stress—exercising, reading, meditating, spending time with close friends and family, etc. Have a plan and employ it regularly.

## The "Me Time" Connection

It may seem counterintuitive, but preserving time for yourself will improve your time with others. In our fast-paced and wired society, it can be hard to get a few moments to yourself. But taking "me" time will help you recharge mentally, emotionally, and spiritually and will aid you in bringing a more positive outlook to your relationships, making it easier to build trust. If finding time for yourself is hard, try waking up a few minutes before the rest of the household. Use your me time for something you enjoy doing, like reading a book, engaging in a sport, going for a walk, or playing a musical instrument. Unplug from your electronic devices during that time to get the maximum benefit. Do this consistently to allow yourself a known reprieve. Just like you schedule your work and have allotted times for meetings, schedule in time for yourself every day, even if it is only fifteen minutes. You cannot take care of others if you have not taken care of yourself. Time set aside to protect your well-being is critical in ensuring you are at your best when dealing with others.

## The Social Connection

Screens are ubiquitous in our society. Everywhere, people are accessing them: at the airport, the bus stop, the grocery line. Social media promises to make us feel more connected and is a large part of what we're accessing. There is some evidence, although not yet conclusive, that social media addiction is real. Studies also show spending large blocks of time on social media can create feelings of sadness and social isolation, and trigger feelings of jealousy and other negative mental states. In-person interactions are decreasing as well. As a result, feelings of sadness and loneliness can increase.[69]

Over half of Americans say they feel lonely.[70] Twenty-five percent report they have no one to confide in.[71] Thirty-six million people in the United States live alone.[72] Loneliness is fast becoming a major disease with severe health and wellness impacts. Unless it's part of your job, limit your scrolling through social media feeds, and instead feed on face-to-face social interactions that are much more real and satisfying and will help build solid trust. Be intentional about participating in activities that will allow you to have healthy interactions: join a book club or recreational sports team, volunteer with a community group or your church, or help a neighbor in need. Create breaks from electronics during meals or other family times of the day. Reach out to others with no purpose other than to connect—people aren't projects. These small interactions can have a meaningful impact on your health and relationships and can also demonstrate to those you love that they are your priority.

## The Nutrition Connection

Mental health studies demonstrate that the fuel we put into our bodies affects our mental health. Drinking insufficient water, for example, can cause fatigue, negative moods, and difficulty concentrating. Consider how you feel when you haven't eaten for a long period of time: lightheaded, tired, irritable, and impatient. Does that sound like someone who lives a trust-filled life? Or think of how you feel when you've eaten too much: disengaged, sluggish, and apathetic. Doesn't sound like someone living a life with a focus on engaging others.

Treat your daily meals with the same organizational approach that you do your daily schedule. Plan ahead and ensure you drink sufficient water. Plan your meals weekly so that you can appropriately address your dietary needs. A diet high in refined, sugary, fried foods, too much meat and high-fat dairy products increases the risk for depression.[73] Plan a balanced diet to include more vegetables, beans, whole grains, greens, fruits, and nuts to give your body the nutrients it needs for your mind to function well and your mood to be more positive.

## Building Healthy Habits

You may have noticed a common theme as we reviewed each of the fundamental behaviors listed above. The tools we identified are all about forming good habits that lead to a healthy lifestyle and happier you. You may already have some positive habits that you use every day, but there is always room for improvement. It is easier to develop good habits when we fully understand the factors behind habit formation.

James Clear lists four laws of behavior change that are core strategies to build good habits: make it obvious, make it attractive, make it easy, and make it satisfying. The opposite holds true when breaking bad habits: make your cues invisible, make your habits unappealing, make the routine as difficult as possible, and make your habit unsatisfying.[74] As you review the behaviors we believe are fundamental to building strong relationships and consider your own answers on how you are currently doing in these areas, Clear's rules can help you shape better habits.

It takes intentionality to improve our behaviors and work toward becoming the best version of ourselves.

## The Health Benefits of Faith

Certain aspects of our well-being are affected by how we define our meaning. Many studies show how our outlook, as defined by our faith/ spirituality, has a positive impact on our health. Dr. Harold Koenig, in his book *Medicine, Religion, and Health*, notes the following:

> It appears that psychological and social factors influence the physiological systems of the body that are directly responsible for good health and the ability to fight disease. Therefore, if religious/spiritual involvement can be shown to enhance psychological health and social interactions, it is reasonable to hypothesize that religious factors may improve physical health as well, doing so by reducing psychological stress, increasing social support, and encouraging positive health behaviors.[75]

A growing body of research demonstrates a positive relationship between faith, medical outcomes, and quality of life. A review of the research conducted in this area produces a multitude of articles and scholarly reports. Consider these findings:

- African American women who employed prayer as a method of coping with racism experienced improved cardiovascular health.[76]
- Patients with advanced cancer who read or listened to spiritual writings reported lower pain levels, increased hope, and a greater sense of well-being.[77]
- People who identified with a religious group exhibited fewer depressive symptoms.[78]
- Those who engaged in private prayer exhibited a significantly decreased frequency of depression.[79]
- Those with a greater level of spirituality experienced less lifetime depression, and fewer suicidal thoughts and behaviors, alcohol use disorders, and incidents of post-traumatic stress disorder.[80]
- Patients with advanced stages of cancer who experienced high spiritual well-being exhibited more positive mood states, higher self-esteem, and an overall better quality of life.[81]

It is important that medical providers recognize this in the care of their patients.

- Healthcare professionals who encourage patients to search for meaning in misfortune may help their quality of life.[82]
- Focusing on the patient's spirituality and spiritual needs can have a positive effect on their health-related quality of life, mental health, and life expectancy. [83]
- Having a strong personal religious belief produces beneficial outcomes to one's health over the long term.[84]

As you can see, many researchers are finding a positive link between faith, medical outcomes, and quality of life. Outcomes worth considering for your own health journey.

## Reflection

1. Have you ever done something out of the ordinary (like jumping in a pool while fully clothed) to shock your system and reset your perspective? How did you feel afterwards?

2. Which of the healthy connections do you feel you have the best handle on? Which is your weakest?

3. Why do you think there is a strong connection between health and faith?

*CHAPTER ELEVEN*

# MY PERSONAL EARTHQUAKE

*"You could leave life right now.*
*Let that determine what you do and say and think."*
~Marcus Aurelius

*he Trust Transformation* is a culmination of significant work done over nearly twenty years. In the opening story, we looked at the 1964 Alaska earthquake and how the impact of that event shifted the state fifty feet, permanently altering the landscape. This illustrates how monumental events can knock us from a place of familiarity and comfort to which we can never return. We can all expect to face earth-shaking moments in our lives. The way we prepare and respond to them determines our well-being and ability to flourish. The transformative power of trust can fortify our spirit and our relationships, lending us resilience during transitions and strength to thrive in new situations.

On May 25, 2019, I (Roy) experienced my own earthquake—an aortic dissection that should have killed me. It completely and irrevocably moved my personal landscape.

When you write a book or create a training program, your prayer is that it will truly help people move where they need to be; that it will put them in a stronger place to deal with issues, confront challenges, and live a better life. You never imagine that the program you wrote will come into play when you face your own mortality.

What seemed like a normal Friday night—dinner with my wife, Kim, at our favorite local sports bar, shopping at Home Depot for some things for the house, and watching a movie on Netflix—would forever change everything. After finishing one movie, Kim decided to go to bed. I wanted to stay up and watch a second one. As is often the case, I fell asleep on the couch before the end of the film.

At 2:00 AM Saturday morning, I woke up with the worst pain I had ever experienced. It was as if somebody was punching a hole in my chest and squeezing the life out of my heart. I got up, hurried to the bedroom, and told Kim, "Get your shoes on. I need you to drive me to the emergency room. I think I'm having a heart attack."

As we made our way to the hospital, I had a stroke and became completely nonresponsive. When we arrived at the emergency room, Kim had to go inside, get a nurse to come out, and help her drag me out of the car and into the room where the medical staff would begin doing their assessment. During the exam, one of the nurses realized that I had no feeling in my arms or legs and told the team he thought they should stop and roll me back to the CT scanner, because he believed I might be having an acute aortic dissection.

An acute aortic dissection is when the aorta, the body's largest artery, begins to split open. Most people that experience an acute aortic dissection aren't able to get help quickly enough. In fact, a good portion of people just die in their sleep. I was very fortunate to have made it to the hospital, where, with the right interventions, there was the possibility of it being repaired.

The emergency department team confirmed the diagnosis. The aorta was splitting open, and it was severe, going from the carotid arteries up near the neck down through the root of the aorta, in the belly. They rapidly called for an air transport to take me to AdventHealth Orlando, the quaternary hospital in the system.

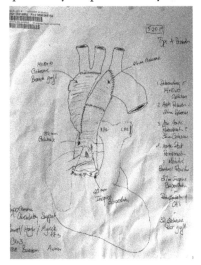

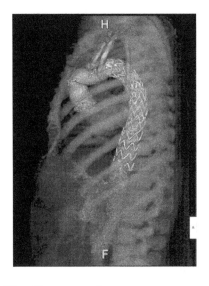

At AdventHealth Orlando, Dr. Clay Burnett and a team were preparing for emergency open heart surgery. I arrived, and they immediately put my body into a steadier state by freezing me so that everything would slow down. During this part of the surgery my heart had to be stopped; this reduced the utilization of my organs and placed them in a better position for recovery.

The surgery lasted six hours. Dr. Burnett said that my case had the most extensive damage possible for such a situation. A significant amount of my aorta had to be replaced with synthetic material during the course of the surgery. Because the damage was so severe and the surgery took such a long time, my organs had to go an extended period without oxygen. The decision was made to put me into an induced coma to help foster recovery.

My chances of living were markedly better post-surgery, but there was still a lot of doubt. I faced the real possibility that if I survived, I would need 24/7 nursing care, because I would be forever damaged by the lack of oxygen to my brain and other organs. There was no reasonable prognosis for a positive outcome.

For a week, I remained in a coma while doctors and nurses monitored my progress. Day after day, small signals of healing were observed. Signs such as the function of my kidneys and other organs began to look a little more promising.

While in my coma, I appeared to be completely immobile, but my brain didn't stop working. My thoughts and emotions throughout that time were vivid and wild. I felt an overwhelming sense of frustration and dread because I couldn't locate my family. I wound up in places where I was either trapped, restrained, or incapacitated—unable to get where I needed to go. At a subconscious level, I must have been aware I was in the hospital, because a lot of my frenzied dreams were set in hospital beds or clinical situations. In addition, I had other experiences where I saw and spoke to friends who had passed on some time ago.

The most prominent of these moments was a talk I had with a fraternity brother named Rod Durham, who had died a few years earlier. The conversation was long, and many of the details are lost to me now. However, I clearly remember Rod reaching over, putting his hand on me, and saying, "It's okay." At that very moment, I woke up.

Waking from a coma after seven days is a bit like waking up in the middle of a plane crash. There are noises, bells, and alarms. You are hooked to all sorts of machines and monitors. You have a doctor, you have nurses, you have your wife, and others all over the bed and in your face telling you to calm down. You're paranoid. For the last seven days, you've been trapped in strange places. Held against your will. Unable to find your family. The chaos you wake to is eerily familiar.

Eventually you calm down and begin to settle. Over the course of the next forty-eight hours, the doctor explains what happened. The nurses describe your recovery. Your wife fills in the details. Your kids come and talk to you too. And everything begins to normalize . . . except for the scar that goes all the way down the front of your chest . . . and the synthetic material piecing your aorta together . . . and the new valve in your heart keeping you alive.

Finding a new normal wasn't easy for me. I faced a long road of recovery. The first hurdle I had to overcome was trusting myself to do what needed to be done for healing. I didn't want to leave the hospital. I felt safe there. People were taking care of me. I didn't have to worry about reopening the incisions in my chest or doing the wrong activities or eating the wrong food.

I had to learn to trust myself again. And, I had to trust others to teach me how.

Once more, my healthcare team proved themselves trustworthy. I received coaching from the cardiovascular ICU nurses, then physical rehab, cardio rehab, and occupational therapy. I learned the importance of flushing my body with fluids and the need for good nutrition and exercise. I was taught how emotional, mental, and spiritual wholeness all play a part in recovery.

Near-death experiences have a way of making one see life through a much clearer lens. I found myself examining places where I had fallen short as a father, a husband, and in my role at work. I wanted to be sure

I was living to my highest potential, and to commit to making things better than they were before. I 'd been given the gift of survival, but surviving was no longer enough. I wanted to THRIVE.

As I left the hospital and began my new life, I knew I had to make significant changes. I doubled down on integrity, consistency, and intentionality in my relationships. I paid more attention to how I spent my time, what I ate, how much I moved my body, and how I incorporated some new non-negotiables—prayer, journaling, meaningful conversations, etc.—into my schedule. In short, I changed how I managed my life.

Again, I had help. The most important team in all of this was my family: my wife, my three sons, and my daughter. We worked—and are still working—to ensure that we were living the way we should be; that our integrity was unassailable; that we were making good decisions for our physical, spiritual, mental, and emotional health; and that we prioritized the relationships that needed to be front and center. (Part of that mental and emotional health came from extending grace to myself when I wasn't able to complete all that I wanted to do.)

Accountability is key to making and sustaining positive changes. One of the lessons I learned during the twelve-week cardiac rehab was that the heart craves exercise, and a consistent exercise routine will lower blood pressure and provide a foundation for other health outcomes, including weight loss. To hold myself accountable, I began posting pictures and regular updates on my experience, walks, and races. The habit became a celebration of life to me (I still count each day since that fateful moment) and a means of encouraging others. As my commitment to exercise—and walking in particular—grew, I began to lean into the power of influence. I participated in a series of 5K events, completed two half marathons, and served as an ambassador for the Track Shack Run Series.

At times, we all need encouragement to trust ourselves enough to take the steps necessary to transform our lives. God has provided me a platform to reach others. Through my story, posts, and races, I've been honored to earn the trust of many people and use my influence to motivate whomever I can. Quite often, someone will go out of their way to share a kind word or thank me for my message and tell me how it's inspired them to act. Playing a part in another person's transformation is a humbling and magnificent gift. Through the transformative power of trust, I've turned my trauma into a message, and it's been the core of my recovery and resilience. Don't ever let your influence go to waste!

In 2022, I participated in my first half marathon and will have completed four by the time this book is published. This was only possible because of the trust I had in myself and the relationship with many others who helped guide and support me. Now I'm responsible for sharing this story to encourage others.

As I think about my earthquake and the factors that played into my experience, I can't help reflecting on the high level of trust among all the people that cared for me. Had the nurse not felt safe speaking up, for instance, and saying, "This is an aortic dissection. Let's stop doing everything else and get him back to the CT," there may have been a delay. Any slowdown could have cost me my life.

I see the work of mission, medicine, and miracles in my story. The extraordinary mission of the healthcare system created a culture of trust and enabled a process that allowed me to be expertly treated, saved, and healed. The medical knowledge and skills of an incredible team of people played a huge part as well. Finally, several miraculous and critical moments of timing can only be explained by providential intervention.

It may sound strange, perhaps even crazy, but what was truly a near-death experience is the best thing that ever happened to me. I live each day as if it were my last, making sure that I pour everything into it and have no regrets.

Confronting my mortality crystalized and simplified my own credo: Love people, be grateful, give generously, and make a difference. This is my trust contract with myself, and it drives everything I do. It has transformed meaning in my life.

## The Power of Meaning

Friedrich Nietzsche once declared, "He who has a 'why' to live for can bear almost any 'how.'" This thought expresses a truth about the power of faith, in that through faith many of us are able to find our meaning, or the "why" for our lives.

In our discussion of attitude in chapter 5, we reviewed some of the insights of concentration camp survivor, psychiatrist, and neurologist Viktor Frankl in his book *Man's Search for Meaning*. What Frankl says about purpose is critical as well. His book is perhaps one of the most influential writings on the topic.

Dr. Frankl observed that those who survived even amid the horrors of the concentration camp were those who felt they had control over their environment. He explained:

> *We who lived in concentration camps can remember the men who walked through the huts comforting others, giving away their last piece of bread. They may have been few in number, but they offer sufficient proof that everything can be taken from a man but one thing: the last of human freedoms—to choose one's own attitude in any given set of circumstances—to choose one's own way.*[85]

An article in *Psychology Today* reviews some of the book's most relevant points about the power of meaning.

> *Frankl's message is ultimately one of hope: even in the most absurd, painful, and dispiriting of circumstances, life can be given a meaning, and so too can suffering. Life in the concentration camp taught Frankl that our main drive or motivation in life is neither pleasure, as Freud had believed, nor power, as Adler had believed, but meaning.*
>
> *According to Frankl, meaning can be found through:*

- *Experiencing reality by interacting authentically with the environment and with others,*
- *Giving something back to the world through creativity and self-expression, and*
- *Changing our attitude when faced with a situation or circumstance that we cannot change.*[86]

Martin Seligman, Fox Leadership Professor of Psychology at the University of Pennsylvania and author of *Flourish*, concludes that the happiest life is one with a true sense of meaning. He states, "The Meaningful Life consists in belonging to and serving something that you believe is bigger than the self."[87] He observes that the pursuit of meaning, not the pursuit of pleasure, is the strongest factor in increasing your life satisfaction.

## Seeking Meaning versus Happiness

All of us need to know that we are contributing to something and making a difference in the world, despite our shortcomings. Many studies in the field of psychology have shown that meaning, and not happiness, is the goal we should pursue to have a more fulfilling, relevant life.[88] One important aspect of faith is that we trust in someone or something bigger than ourselves. This trust then provides a framework to find our meaning in life and can bring purpose to the work we do.

Emily Esfahani Smith writes about the importance of finding purpose in life in *The Power of Meaning*. In her popular book and TED Talk, she points out that while our modern culture is focused on obtaining happiness, meaning is absent from many people's lives. At the same time, we see an increase in the US suicide rates, currently at a thirty-year high despite the improvements in most quality-of-life indicators. She writes, "Even though life is getting objectively better by nearly every conceivable standard, more people feel hopeless, depressed, and alone."

Esfahani Smith illustrates the concept of meaning with four pillars:

1. **Belonging**—being in loving relationships where you value one another.
2. **Purpose**—the "why" that drives you forward, defined as less about what you want and more about what you give.
3. **Transcendence**—being lifted above the hustle and bustle of daily life so that you feel connected to a higher reality.
4. **Storytelling**—the story you tell yourself about yourself, recognizing that you are the author of your story.[89]

## The Power of Faith

We've learned that our interpersonal relationships can be much more productive and fulfilling when we are more intentional about building trust first, last, and always. We improve our results as we improve relationships.

Now we want to explore the ultimate form of trust that gives meaning to life and creates an even greater impact on us and those around us—our trust in God. Faith affects every aspect of our being. In the previous chapter, we discussed the positive health effects of practicing faith. However, the advantages of an active faith life extend beyond general health benefits. Those with active faith lives have greater strength in times of difficulty, more assurance in important decision-making, a clearer purpose in life, and a greater calling to help others.

The last few decades have seen an abundance of research on faith and its effect on emotional, relational, and physical health. In *The Healing Power of Faith*, Dr. Harold Koenig cites several studies that show, among other things, that . . .

- *Those with a committed faith who also participate in a faith community are more likely to experience greater emotional well-being and happiness, lower stress levels, and better postoperative recovery outcomes than the general population.*

- *Those with deep religious faith have less likelihood of experiencing depression from stressful events in their lives.*
- *Those who practice their faith by prayer, attending religious services, and regular Bible reading have lower diastolic blood pressure than those who do not.*
- *Those who experience illness and who have a strong faith recuperate more quickly than those who are not religious.*
- *Those who regularly attend religious meetings have stronger immune systems than those who do not.*[90]

One study, led by Jeffrey Levin, PhD, concluded that "the more religious faith people had, the greater their life satisfaction. Amazingly, not only was this a strong determinant of well-being—it was a stronger determinant than age and even health."[91]

We recognize that faith is the ultimate personal belief. Not all people look to a higher power or seek this kind of trust relationship. Regardless of where you find yourself, there are health and well-being benefits of faith that you really should consider.

## The Role of Faith in a High-Stakes Profession

I (Omayra) believe the role of faith in a high-stakes profession like healthcare is important, not only because healthcare is my field, but because sooner or later, it is something that will affect us all.

At first glance, it may be difficult to understand that faith serves a key role in our overall health and in the delivery of healthcare by physicians and other providers. Generally speaking, physicians are scientists, taught in medical school the importance of evidence-based medicine that has developed over decades of scientific research and discovery. In reality, however, physicians are human beings who are blessed and plagued at the same time with all the characteristics that each of us are capable of. They are at risk of making errors despite all their best intentions to do no harm. They rejoice with patients in times of gladness and suffer with their patients and families during times of illness and death. It is to their benefit and that of their patients that physicians consider the role of faith and spirituality as they deliver healthcare.

In the preceding section, we addressed the benefits that having high spirituality, practicing prayer, and identifying oneself as religious can have on a person's physical and psychological well-being. Now let's consider the perspective of the medical provider caring for patients in their healthcare journey.

In the article "The Role of Spirituality in Healthcare," Dr. Christina Puchalski describes the importance of medical providers being compassionate, and defines the word compassion as "to suffer with." She notes that "compassionate care calls physicians to walk with people in the midst of their pain." Every day, physicians care for patients who are dealing with different challenges in their lives: chronic diseases, new pregnancies, illnesses in children and the elderly, and terminal diagnoses, to name a few. Additionally, those seeking end-of-life care have a multitude of questions they may want to ask, such as, "Why is this happening to me now? What will happen to me after I die? Is there a God?" The impact these diagnoses can have on a patient's emotional and psychological well-being can be tempered by the role of spirituality in their life. Cure is not possible for many illnesses, but . . . there is always room for healing.

As healthcare providers, physicians can use knowledge of a patient's spiritual beliefs to help determine clinical interventions. In her article, Dr. Puchalski advises providers to practice compassionate presence and listen to patients. She also recommends obtaining a spiritual history and incorporating appropriate spiritual practices into a patient's plan of care.[92]

As an emergency physician, I (Omayra) am faced with moments of crisis daily. We make life-and-death decisions that will have a lasting impact on our patients and their families. I have found that incorporating faith into my personal and professional life has been essential to my own growth and well-being, and to my ability to continue to practice medicine. Practicing compassionate care allows me to cultivate trust when seconds count. Learning about the spiritual needs and wishes of my patients helps me direct their medical care in a manner that demonstrates that I respect them as an individual. It is a great honor when I am asked by a patient or their family to pray with them. I know we have established a high level of trust and understanding in our doctor-patient relationship that should create better medical outcomes.

We thrive on interpersonal relationships, and during times of illness these relationships take on even more importance and are critical to deepening trust. Take a moment to consider how faith and spirituality have played a role in your health or a specific healthcare experience.

Spirituality is not only important in the field of healthcare. Studies show that incorporating spiritual values into the workplace can translate into greater productivity and profitability, as well as greater customer loyalty and employee retention. Some companies provide time for prayer, a quiet room for meditation and stress release, or "lunch and learn" religious programming for their employees.[93] In every walk of life, embracing spirituality and meaning can provide a benefit to your relationships by enhancing trust transformations.

## Five Faith-Developing Practices

Depending where you find yourself on the journey of faith, there are many ways to exercise and grow faith, find meaning, and make a difference in your life and in the lives of others.

Let's examine five practices that can help you grow your faith as part of your trust transformation:

### 1. Plug into the Power of Prayer

Prayer has been shown to impact well-being in several measurable ways. In a *Psychology Today* article, Clay Routledge, PhD, lists five scientifically supported benefits of prayer:

- *Prayer improves self-control.* A study found that those who prayed before trying to perform a task exhibited greater self-control than those who did not. Prayer allowed them to maintain better control of their emotions.
- *Prayer makes you nicer.* A series of studies demonstrated that a benevolent prayer for a person who has made you angry is effective in reducing the anger and aggression you feel.
- *Prayer makes you more forgiving.* Researchers discovered that participants who prayed for their partner or friend who hurt them were more likely to forgive that partner or friend.
- *Prayer increases trust.* Researchers found that people who pray together with a close friend or partner had a greater sense of unity with that person. Dr. Routledge stated, "Social prayer may thus help build close relationships."
- *Prayer offsets the negative health effects of stress.* Study subjects who prayed prayers of thanks or to get closer to God experienced higher measures of subjective well-being, including self-esteem, optimism, meaning, and satisfaction with life.[94]

## 2. Make the Self-Reflection Connection

In the previous chapter, we suggested taking a daily "me" break in order to recharge mentally, emotionally, and spiritually and to escape for a while from life's bustle. Some experts suggest setting aside time, at least once a week, for introspection and to gain personal insight.

*Self-reflection* is "serious thought about your own character and actions."[95] Many religions or faith traditions see this as an integral part of the spiritual journey. As difficult as it might be, we all need to examine our motives, behaviors, and attitudes regularly so that we learn more about what makes us tick and what we can improve upon. This can lead to spiritual growth and, occasionally, a spiritual breakthrough.

You may wonder, *Isn't that narcissistic?* It isn't. If you are taking time to look at yourself for the purpose of self-improvement, the time you take will help you grow and become a better, more trustworthy person. That will benefit not only you, but everyone around you.

Kick-start your self-reflection by creating a list of thoughtful questions to answer. You could also begin by thinking of difficult situations or persons in your life and building solutions for dealing with them. You might use your self-reflection time to uncover wrong thinking or poor attitudes on your part, or bad relationships that you need to cut off. You may want to examine yourself to ensure you are living up to your own values and personal mission. Taking time for self-reflection will help you approach life intentionally and not haphazardly. This is essential for building trust.

## 3. Change Your Perspective

We all face difficult situations in our personal or professional lives. It can be challenging to understand another person's opinion if it goes contrary to our own. If my focus is purely on selfish ends, I might be tempted to stick with my own viewpoint and disregard the other person's opinion entirely. However, a faith perspective calls me to a place of humility, a place where I must lay value on the viewpoint of others.

It's been said that your perspective can vary depending on "where you sit in the room." When facing an impasse with someone whose viewpoint is quite different from yours, humbly try to "sit in that person's seat" to gain their perspective. Seeing the room from their view may help you understand the nature of the disagreement and reframe your reaction accordingly. Ask yourself right now, is there someone that I need to be more empathetic with regarding their perspective or situation?

## 4. Focus on Positives, Not Negatives

When relationships are strained or circumstances are difficult, it is easy to focus on the negative. However, doing so often leads to a downward spiral of emotional energy, poor communication with others, and broken trust. To counter this tendency, focus on finding something positive in the situation.

There is truth to the adage "every cloud has a silver lining." Seek to find that silver lining amid bad circumstances. Try keeping a gratitude journal. Each day, write down three specific things that went well and for which you are grateful. Being positive doesn't mean you ignore the negative; it simply means you have faith that a good outcome is not only possible but worth striving for.

### 5. Practice Grace Daily

Experientially, we all know "to err is human." Faith teaches that none of us is perfect and all of us need grace and forgiveness at some point. This is hard to remember, however, when someone treats you unfairly. What to do? When you feel wronged, take a deep breath and remember *no one is perfect*! You have an opportunity to practice grace and forgive those who have hurt or betrayed you. Allowing others that moment of grace gives you the freedom to move on and release negative feelings that may ultimately drag you down.

## Reflection

1. Have you had your own earthshaking moment that forever changed your life? Has something good come of it?

2. Are you clear on the purpose of your life?

3. Were you surprised by all of the benefits of faith? Are there ways you would like to try to grow your faith?

# CHAPTER TWELVE

# COMMIT TO TRUST

*"Unless commitment is made,*
*there are only promises and hopes; but no plans."*
~Peter Drucker

How committed are you to your relationships? In marriage, we have a ceremony, share vows, and file papers with the government—essentially making marriage a contractual relationship. What steps might we take to demonstrate our commitment to putting trust at the center of all our relationships?

## Put It in Writing

To master anything, you must practice and keep the discipline you are working on at top of mind. We create tools, lists, mission statements, and monuments to ideas that we want to remember and move forward. A written commitment is a particularly vital tool that will make a significant difference in the results you see.

Research supports taking immediate action on an idea to ensure its success. In an article entitled "Using Commitment as a Tool to Promote Behavior Change in Extension Programming"[96] published in the *Journal of Extension*, the authors cited studies that demonstrated the impact of making commitments and, in particular, making them in writing.

- "Individuals who commit to a small action are likely to commit to something bigger."
- "While public commitments appear more effective than private commitments, those commitments that are public and durable are likely to be particularly effective."[97]
- "When individuals make a commitment, they are more likely to follow through with their promise to ensure that the commitment is maintained."[98]

## Building a Trust Tribe

My (Roy's) original course, *Outrageous Trust*, was primarily targeted to leaders to help build and foster a culture of trust within their organizations. The success of those early engagements encouraged us to build a program that went much deeper into each individual's overall well-being.

Some of the initial adopters have continued to use the program. They have seen incredible outcomes as a result of their commitment to being intentional about trust in their relationships. One of the tools that we incorporated into the training was a written commitment by participants to a set of trust-building principles. Each organization personalized the contract/creed to fit the culture and personality of its company. These three examples provide insight into the power of trust and the benefits of codifying a commitment to foster trust in all that we do.

## Wendy Brandon, CEO, UCF Medical Center at Lake Nona

As CEO of Central Florida Regional Medical Center, Wendy Brandon had her leadership group participate in a daylong training of *Outrageous Trust*. The team drafted a contract and, over the weeks that followed, they revised and agreed on the principles. Once finalized, each of the executives signed the contract. In addition to the copies they were all given, a large version of the document was framed and hung in the human resources office, to serve as a monument to the leadership team's commitment to trust.

This commitment was renewed every time another member of the team was hired. Two executives would invite the new member to lunch, share the contract and explain its use, then, along with the new employee, sign the agreement. All team members would sign the latest contract. Fresh copies of the new document would be sent to everyone.

Wendy observed that the trust contract provided a connection among her team members, which kept turnover down and strengthened the organization's culture. It also provided a great tool for addressing issues and keeping relationships in perspective when challenges arose.

## Pam Nabors, CEO, CareerSource Central Florida

Appointed CEO to CareerSource Central Florida (an agency that provides employment and community workforce services), Pam Nabors was charged with rebuilding an organization that had been shut down by Florida's governor for misappropriation of funds and other issues that damaged the organization.

The challenge was overwhelming. To set a baseline for the company's reputation, Pam solicited the help of the UCF College of Business to conduct a survey of the community. While working with UCF, Pam had her executive team go through the *Outrageous Trust* program.

They drafted what they called their "Trust Creed." Once the creed was adopted, Pam had her entire staff of more than two hundred team members participate in an abbreviated version of the program. The team at each work location was asked to develop its own Trust Creed based on the one adopted by the executive team.

Pam says that the creed has provided a foundation for the organization's culture. It has defined behavior, set expectations, and positively influenced how conflicts are resolved. Today, CareerSource Central Florida is one of the most respected organizations of its kind nationwide and among the most admired of community organizations in Central Florida. As workforce becomes an increasingly volatile issue, CareerSource Central Florida is expanding its capacity and resources to serve their communities. The now-trusted organization continues to be asked by leaders in both the business and government sectors to take on new and important roles. Additionally, all team members from CareerSource Central Florida now go through *The Trust Transformation* program.

## Russ Suddeth, Former CEO, Co-founder, J. Raymond Construction

J. Raymond Construction is a general contracting company located in Longwood, Florida. The firm specializes in the development and construction of retail locations. Its clients include Walmart, Publix, and The Fresh Market. Founded in 1988 by Russ Suddeth and John Sofarelli, the firm now builds around $200 million in projects annually. Throughout its history, J. Raymond Construction has been a stable and highly reputable firm with steady growth over the first twenty years.

During the housing market crash that began in 2007 and sent the country into an economic tailspin, J. Raymond Construction saw its revenue drop from nearly $150 million to $50 million. Leadership had to take action to keep their team intact. Unlike many who just laid off staff, Russ and John committed to keeping everyone employed with benefits. They had to reduce salaries to accomplish this, but they kept their commitment.

Coming out of the recession, the firm was able to hit the ground running as the market rebounded. Part of what made—and still makes—J. Raymond so consistent and resilient was its commitment to values that define its culture. Russ says, "We do business the RIGHT way. It's an acronym, where each letter sets an expectation for how we behave and work. R is respect, I is integrity, G is the Golden Rule, H is humility, and the last letter, T, is trust."

By 2013, the company had recovered much of its market share with revenues of nearly $100 million. It was at this point that the company's founders introduced the *Outrageous Trust* program to their team members. Russ said, "John and I were contemplating our exit from the company. We had identified the key people that would buy us out and wanted to be sure we were setting them up for success, so we turned to this program to fortify our culture." All the employees went through the training. Over the next few weeks, J. Raymond developed its own trust contract for everyone to sign. Not only did the contract become the code of behavior for everyone, it also provided a framework for addressing differences and disputes. Russ explained, "Whenever someone would come to me with a problem they had with someone else, I would pull out the contract and we'd look at how specifically they should deal with it."

At the time Russ and John executed their buyout in 2019, the company was performing better than ever. It continued to grow in the years that followed. In the period since the trust contract was adopted (to the time of this writing), 75 percent of the employee team have remained.

## Trust Contracts in the Workplace

The above stories illustrate that organizations focused on trust can achieve incredible results. If you want to put trust at the center of your team's relationships, a contract or credo is a powerful tool. Below, you will find a list of credos to consider. Choose from them, adjust them, or let them inspire you and your team as you work together to build a trust contract that fits your needs. If you are interested in having your organization participate in *The Trust Transformation* four-hour course, visit www.TheTrustTransformation.com.

**Sample Commitments for a Trust Contract:**
- I will act with integrity in everything I do, in public and in private.
- I will choose my attitude each day. With humility, I will take responsibility for my relationships, seek help from others, and be mindful of all the little things I do that contribute to or diminish trust with others.
- I will treat everyone with respect by listening first and communicating consistently with openness and candor.
- I will foster a culture that models forgiveness and provides "safe zones" where people can freely and confidently speak to address issues and opportunities.
- I will provide a consistent, reliable experience, "closing the loop" and offering follow-up that helps others be dependable in their roles and responsibilities.
- I will exceed expectations and demonstrate perseverance even through the most difficult situations.
- I will strive to create unity by breaking down any silos that exist which may keep my team from meeting its goals and objectives.
- I will be a positive ambassador for those I represent, in words and in deeds.
- I will immediately stop and address gossip, holding those I interact with to a higher degree of accountability.

## Your Personal Contract

How will you exercise an intentional and mindful approach to earning, building, cultivating, repairing, and restoring trust in your relationships on a daily basis?

We suggest you start with a personal contract and an action plan. For your contract, choose ten affirmative statements that describe how you will exercise greater intentionality in building and repairing trust. Many of the above examples can be used or modified to fit your personal trust contract.

When you are finished, sign your contract, post it somewhere you will notice daily (bathroom mirror, office wall, refrigerator . . .), and tell someone who will hold you accountable.

You might want to model your contract after this example, which includes the four attributes and guiding principles of transformational trust:

## My Personal Trust Transformation Contract

I, _____, will work every day to follow these guiding principles to ensure I am focused on building fulfilling, productive relationships:

A. Be trustworthy and take responsibility for my relationships.
B. Be authentic and build trust from the inside out.
C. Be dependable and communicate consistently.
D. Be influential and a good steward of my trust.

To accomplish this goal, I will commit to the following steps that will guide my actions in engaging with people to earn transformational trust, improving my relationships to improve the results.

1. I will act with integrity in everything I do, in public and in private, ensuring the safety and care for the best interests of those with whom I am entrusted to work for and work with.
2. I will choose my attitude each day. With humility, I will take responsibility for each relationship, seek help from others, and be mindful of all the little things I do that contribute to or diminish trust with everyone.

3. I will be kind to myself.

(And so on . . .)

10. I will immediately stop and address gossip. I will hold myself and others to a higher degree of accountability.

Signed: _____

Date: _____

## Trust Transformation Action Plan

In addition to a commitment, real change requires a plan. Daily journaling and meditation are good lifelong habits to develop (if you haven't already). For the next twelve weeks, we'd like you to follow a simple, daily pattern of questioning, reflecting, and journaling that will lead to dramatic changes in your relationship with yourself and others. During the twelve weeks, you will work your way through the four attributes and guiding principles at each level of the trust circles, beginning with "me," then moving to "we," then "us."

- ❏ WEEK 1: "Me" Trustworthy: Take Responsibility for Your Relationships
- ❏ WEEK 2: "Me" Authentic: Build Trust from the Inside Out
- ❏ WEEK 3: "Me" Dependable: Keep Your Promises and Communicate Consistently
- ❏ WEEK 4: "Me" Influential: Be a Good Steward of Your Trust
- ❏ WEEK 5: "We" Trustworthy: Take Responsibility for Your Relationships
- ❏ WEEK 6: "We" Authentic: Build Trust from the Inside Out
- ❏ WEEK 7: "We" Dependable: Keep Your Promises and Communicate Consistently
- ❏ WEEK 8: "We" Influential: Be a Good Steward of Your Trust

❑ WEEK 9: "Us" Trustworthy: Take Responsibility for Your Relationships

❑ WEEK 10: "Us" Authentic: Build Trust from the Inside Out

❑ WEEK 11 "Us" Dependable: Keep Your Promises and Communicate Consistently

❑ WEEK 12: "Us" Influential: Be a Good Steward of Your Trust

Find a quiet place (maybe somewhere outside?) and moment of the day to start your trust introspection time. Begin with a deep breath or two to help you focus and to chase away distracting thoughts.

Next, reread your trust commitment so that it stays fresh in your mind.

Then, reflect on and journal about one or two of these questions as they relate to the attribute and circle of trust you are focusing on for each respective week:

ASSESSMENT QUESTIONS:
1. What am I doing well in this area right now?
2. What am I doing poorly in this area right now?
3. How is my reputation being affected by my behavior?

TRANSFORMATION QUESTIONS:
4. What is one good habit I will implement to improve my performance in this area?
5. What is one bad habit I will eliminate to improve my performance in this area?
6. What specific action steps will I take to make improvements in this area?

Finally, ask yourself how well you lived out your trust-building intentions the previous day (or in the time since you last journaled). Be generous with yourself and not embarrassed to write down what you did well. But be honest about shortcomings, too. How could you have done better?

That's it! That's your plan for focusing on trust building in the coming weeks and learning to make the practice of trust-building principles habits for life. Simple, right? Well, maybe not simple, but definitely doable and incredibly worthwhile.

Remember, consistency is key. If you honor your contract and follow your action plan with consistency, you and your relationships will be sure to experience life-changing trust transformations.

*"Excellence is the gradual result*
*of always striving to do better."*
**~Pat Riley**

# SUCCESS STRATEGIES

The following is a quick reference to many of the ideas we have covered to help you build more enriching, trusting relationships.

**BUILD TRUST INTENTIONALLY**
Approach each interaction with an intentionality to build trust by your behavior.

**BE DEPENDABLE AND CONSISTENT**
Be the kind of person that others can depend on to keep promises.

**DO THE RIGHT THING**
Choosing the right path even when no one is looking will give you a clear conscience and help you trust yourself.

**BE PRESENT**
Put away your devices and be an active listener. Focus on the concerns of the person you are with. Be present in the moment.

## RESPECT EVERYONE

Be considerate of others; you don't know what struggles they may be having. Remember the Golden Rule! Treating others with respect fosters trust.

## COMMUNICATE

Boost trust by learning to listen and communicate positively and consistently.

## SPEAK TRUTH

Trust is built when others see you tell the truth regardless of the personal consequences to yourself.

## SHOW GRACE AND HUMILITY

Acknowledge that you aren't perfect, that you can learn from others, and that you need their feedback.

## APOLOGIZE AND FORGIVE

We all make mistakes, but what we do afterwards will either build or erode trust. When you're to blame, apologize sincerely. When you've been hurt, let go of the negative feelings and move on.

## REFRAME ADVERSITY

Adversity is the opportunity to get outside your comfort zone and grow. Reframe the way you view a problem.

## RECORD AND EXPRESS GRATITUDE

Gratitude helps your attitude. Take time to be thankful and be intentional about expressing gratitude to others.

## FIND YOUR PURPOSE

Carve out time regularly to identify and refine your purpose.

## FOCUS ON SERVICE

As you serve others, you will feel great, boost trust in those around you, and have a positive influence on all those who see it. Small acts of kindness can have a big effect.

## USE YOUR INFLUENCE FOR GOOD

Use your influence on behalf of someone else in need. Be intentional. Be the example you want to see.

## TRUST IN GOD

Trusting in someone or something bigger than yourself can help you find meaning. It turns focus away from the transitory nature of life and toward eternal hope for the future.

## PRAY OR MEDITATE

Prayer can help improve your overall health, optimism, trust, quality of life, and mental well-being.

## LOOK UP

Spend time in nature regularly to decompress and gain perspective.

# ABOUT THE AUTHORS

Roy Reid, APR, CPRC, MCPC helps executive leaders and entrepreneurs transform from states of frustration, overwhelm, and burnout, caused by low-trust relationships and their consequences — high turnover, inefficiencies, poor outcomes, broken marriages, and anxiety — to a state of confidence, balance, satisfaction, and focus through the power of trust.

Many refer to Roy as a living miracle. His inspirational story of survival is the foundation for the important message he delivers on the transformational power of trust. In 2019, he was struck down by an acute aortic dissection that most medical professionals say should have ended his life. Instead, it transformed it into a purpose Roy describes as: "love people, be grateful, give generously and make a difference".

Roy is a sought-after speaker and helps leaders develop resilient and courageous teams that foster a high-trust culture where people feel safe, do the right thing, deliver outstanding service, and strive to improve performance each day.

He is currently a Senior Fellow with The Stockworth Institute, working to build an education platform dedicated to providing companies with the competent skilled workforce they need in today's competitive and unstable marketplace. He's been recognized by Trust Across America/Trust Around the World with a lifetime achievement award.

Roy has worked with Fortune 500® companies, healthcare organizations, entrepreneurs, professional service firms, and public agencies. Some of the leading brands include AdventHealth, University of Central Florida, Wal-Mart, CSX Transportation, Stockworth, Tavistock Group, Lake Nona, and Duke Energy.

Roy holds his Bachelor of Science degree in Business Administration from the University of Central Florida. He is an accredited public relations professional (APR), a certified public relations counselor (CPRC) and Master Certified Professional Coach (MCPC). He is also a master martial artist with a fifth-degree black belt in Taekwondo.

**Omayra Mansfield, MD, MHA, FACEP** is board-certified by the American Board of Emergency Medicine and is a Fellow of the American College of Emergency Physicians. Dr. Mansfield completed her medical degree and master's in healthcare administration at the University of Florida and her emergency medicine residency at Carolinas Medical Center in North Carolina.

Prior to working as an emergency medicine physician, Dr. Mansfield spent several years in healthcare administration and has held several leadership roles in various departments throughout her over two-decade career in healthcare, in areas including medical staff, faculty group practice, emergency department, and finance. She has been honored with the ACHE Innovation Award, Resident Research Award, SAEM Excellence in Emergency Medicine Award, and AMA Medical Student Leadership Award, among others.

Dr. Mansfield has a passion for motivating others to achieve a life of health and balance. She regularly speaks to corporate and public groups on topics such as transformational trust in the workplace and improving health and wellness at home and work. She has a keen interest in educating healthcare teams on patient safety and improving the patient experience and has lectured extensively on these topics.

Omayra is also recognized as one of the Top 100 Thought Leaders Influencing Trusted Business Behavior by Trust across America/Trust around the World. She is a contributing author to a number of books, articles, and publications, and teaches people how to improve results by improving relationships through a more intentional focus on earning, building, and restoring trust. She also served as a principal investigator on research studies at AdventHealth to explore the impact and outcomes of a more intentional focus on trust in relationships.

Dr. Mansfield lives in Orlando with her husband and their daughter Elizabeth and son Alexander, where the family enjoys staying active doing CrossFit and running.

For more information or to contact the authors,
visit www.TheTrustTransformation.com

# ENDNOTES

1   "2021 Edelman Trust Barometer," Edelman, accessed November 11, 2022, https://www.edelman.com/trust/2021-trust-barometer.

2   Kelly Piron, "Edelman Trust Barometer 2022—Distrust Is the Default," Edelman, April 29, 2022, https://www.edelman.be/insights/edelman-trust-barometer-2022-distrust-default.

3   "Surveys of Trust in the U.S. Health Care System," NORC at the University of Chicago, May 21, 2021, https://buildingtrust.org/wp-content/uploads/2021/05/20210520_NORC_ABIM_Foundation_Trust-in-Healthcare_Part-1.pdf.

4   Mary Jo Kreitzer, "Why Personal Relationships Are Important," University of Minnesota Taking Charge of Your Health & Wellbeing, accessed November 23, 2022, https://www.takingcharge.csh.umn.edu/why-personal-relationships-are-important.

5   Emma Seppala, "Positive Teams Are More Productive," *Harvard Business Review*, March 18, 2015, https://hbr.org/2015/03/positive-teams-are-more-productive.

6   Jo Shapiro, "Confronting Unprofessional Behavior in Medicine," *British Medical Journal* 360 (March 7, 2018): k1025, https://doi.org/10.1136/bmj.k1025.

7   Michael Brennan and Verna Monson, "Professionalism: Good for Patients and Health Care Organizations," *Mayo Clinic Proceedings* 89, no. 5 (May 2014): 644–52, https://doi.org/10.1016/j.mayocp.2014.01.011; Arieh Riskin et al., "The Impact of Rudeness on Medical Team Performance: A Randomized Trial," *Pediatrics* 136, no. 3 (September 2015); 487–95, https://doi.org/10.1542/peds.2015-1385.

8   Liz Mineo, "Good Genes Are Nice, but Joy Is Better," *The Harvard Gazette*, April 11, 2017, https://news.harvard.edu/gazette/story/2017/04/over-nearly-80-years-harvard-study-has-been-showing-how-to-live-a-healthy-and-happy-life/.

9   Matthew Solan, "The Secret to Happiness? Here's Some Advice from the Longest-Running Study on Happiness," Harvard Health (blog), October 5, 2017, https://www.health.harvard.edu/blog/the-secret-to-happiness-heres-some-advice-from-the-longest-running-study-on-happiness-2017100512543.

10  "1964 Alaska Earthquake," History, updated August 21, 2018, https://www.history.com/topics/natural-disasters-and-environment/1964-alaska-earthquake.

11  "Earthquakes & Tsunamis," Department of Natural Resources, Geological & Geophysical Surveys, accessed November 23, 2022, https://dggs.alaska.gov/popular-geology/earthquakes-tsunamis.html; "The 1964 Great Alaska Earthquake History," Alaska Division of Homeland Security and Emergency Management, updated April 13, 2022, https://ready.alaska.gov/_64Quake/History.

12  *Merriam-Webster Online,* s.v. "trust," accessed November 23, 2022, https://www.merriam-webster.com/dictionary/trust.

13  Luke 16:10 (New International Version).

14  Rick Warren, *The Purpose Driven Life: What on Earth Am I Here For?* (Grand Rapids: Zondervan, 2002), 148.

15  Maia Szalavitz, "Humility: A Quiet, Underappreciated Strength," *TIME,* April 27, 2012, http://healthland.time.com/2012/04/27/humility-a-quiet-underappreciated-strength.

16  Jenitza Luna Quinones, "UCF College of Business Undergraduate Programs Achieve First U.S. News and World Report Ranking," University of Central Florida, accessed November 23, 2022, https://business.ucf.edu/ranked-us-news/.

17  Mineo, "Good Genes Are Nice, but Joy Is Better."

18  Kreitzer, "Why Personal Relationships Are Important."

19  Dan Buettner, "Reverse Engineering Longevity," *Blue Zones,* accessed November 23, 2022, https://www.bluezones.com/2016/11/power-9/.

20  Sheldon Cohen et al., "Sociability and Susceptibility to the Common Cold," *Psychological Science* 14, no. 5 (September 2003): 389–395, https://doi.org/10.1111/1467-9280.01452.

21  G. Oscar Anderson, "Loneliness Among Older Adults: A National Survey of Adults 45+," AARP Research, September 2010, https://www.aarp.org/research/topics/life/info-2014/loneliness_2010.html.

22  Steve Crabtree, "Social Support Linked to Health Satisfaction Worldwide," Gallup, February 17, 2012, https://news.gallup.com/poll/152738/Social-Support-Linked-Health-Satisfaction-Worldwide.aspx.

23  John F. Helliwell and Haifang Huang, "Comparing the Happiness Effects of Real and On-Line Friends," National Bureau of Economic Research, January 2013, https://www.nber.org/system/files/working_papers/w18690/w18690.pdf.

24  Louise Hawkley et al., "Loneliness Predicts Increased Blood Pressure: 5-Year Cross-Lagged Analyses in Middle-Aged and Older Adults." *Psychology and Aging* 25, no. 1 (March 2010): 132–141, https://doi.org/10.1037/a0017805.

25 Kim Cameron et al., "Effects of Positive Practices on Organizational Effectiveness," *The Journal of Applied Behavioral Science* 47, no. 3 (September 2011): 266–308, https://doi.org/10.1177/0021886310395514.

26 Dickson Okello and Lucy Gilson, "Exploring the Influence of Trust Relationships on Motivation in the Health Sector: A Systematic Review," *Human Resources for Health* 13 (March 31, 2015): 16, https//doi.org10.1186/s12960-015-0007-5.

27 Stephen R. Covey, *The 7 Habits of Highly Effective People: Restoring the Character Ethic* (New York: Free Press, 1989), 198.

28 *Merriam-Webster Online*, s.v. "trustworthy," accessed November 25, 2022, httsp://merriam-webster.com/dictionary/trustworthy.

29 *Merriam-Webster's Collegiate Dictionary*, 11th ed. (2020), s.v. "authentic."

30 *Merriam-Webster Online*, s.v. "dependable," accessed November 25, 2022, httsp://merriam-webster.com/dictionary/dependable.

31 *Merriam-Webster Online*, s.v. "influential," accessed November 25, 2022, httsp://merriam-webster.com/dictionary/influential.

32

33 Onora O'Neill, "What We Don't Understand About Trust," filmed June 2013, TEDxHousesOfParliament video, 9:50, https://www.ted.com/talks/onora_o_neill_what_we_don_t_understand_about_trust.

34 *Merriam-Webster Online*, s.v. "integrity," accessed November 25, 2022, httsp://merriam-webster.com/dictionary/integrity.

35 *Merriam-Webster Online*, s.v. "attitude," accessed November 25, 2022, httsp://merriam-webster.com/dictionary/attitude.

36 Travis Bradberry, "Why Attitude Is More Important Than IQ," *Forbes*, January 19, 2016, https://www.forbes.com/sites/travis bradberry/2016/01/19/why-attitude-is-more-important-than-iq/#7661e6023bd0.

ENDNOTES | 183

37 Viktor E. Frankl, *Man's Search for Meaning: An Introduction to Logotherapy* (New York: Beacon Press, 2006), 66.

38 John C. Maxwell, *The Difference Maker: Making Your Attitude Your Greatest Asset* (Nashville: Nelson Business, 2006), 4.

39 Martin Seligman et al., "Positive Psychology Progress: Empirical Validation of Interventions," *The American Psychologist* 60, no. 5 (July–August 2005): 410–421, https://doi.org/10.1037/0003-066X.60.5.410.

40 "Gratitude Letter," Duke University, accessed November 25, 2022, https://duke.qualtrics.com/jfe/form/SV_200ktTwZpgGTi6x?Q_JFE=qdg.

41 Brené Brown, *The Gifts of Imperfection* (New York: Random House, 2020).

42 Don Jernigan, *The Hidden Power of Relentless Stewardship: 5 Keys to Developing a World-Class Organization,* (New York: Rosetta Books, 2016), 161.

43 *Merriam-Webster Online*, s.v. "authentic," accessed November 21, 2017, https://www.merriam-webster.com/dictionary/authentic.

44 Matthew 7:12 (New International Version).

45 Del Jones, "CEOs Say How You Treat a Waiter Can Predict a Lot About Your Character," *USA Today*, April 14, 2006, https://web.archive.org/web/20160325213116/http://usatoday30.usatoday.com/money/companies/ management/2006-04-14-ceos-waiter-rule_x.htm.

46 Albert Mehrabian, *Silent Messages: Implicit Communication of Emotions and Attitudes* (Belmont, CA: Wadsworth Publishing Co., 1972).

47 M. Kim Marvel et al., "Soliciting the Patient's Agenda: Have We Improved?" *Journal of the American Medical Association* 281, no. 3 (January 20, 1999): 283–287, https://doi.org/ 10.1001/ jama.281.3.283.

48 Kelli Swayden et al., "Effect of Sitting vs. Standing on Perception of Provider Time at Bedside: A Pilot Study," *Patient Education and Counseling* 86, no. 2 (2012): 166–71, https://doi.org/10.1016/j.pec.2011.05.024.

49 Jim Collins, *Good to Great: Why Some Companies Make the Leap and Others Don't* (New York: Harper Business, 2011), 83–85.

50 Dick Tibbits, *Forgive to Live: How Forgiveness Can Save Your Life, 10th Anniversary Edition* (Orlando: Florida Hospital Publishing, 2016).

51 Jennifer Latson, "How Poisoned Tylenol Became a Crisis-Management Teaching Model," *TIME,* September 29, 2014, https://time.com/3423136/tylenol-deaths-1982/.

52 Azize Sahin, Cemal Zehir, Hakan Kitapçi, "The Effects of Brand Experiences, Trust and Satisfaction on Building Brand Loyalty; An Empirical Research on Global Brands," *Social and Behavioral Sciences* 24 (2011): 1288–1301, https://doi.org/10.1016/j.sbspro.2011.09.143.

53 James Clear, *Atomic Habits: An Easy & Proven Way to Build Good Habits & Break Bad Ones* (New York: Avery, 2018), 38.

54 Jack Canfield with Janet Switzer, *The Success Principles: How to Get from Where You Are to Where You Want to Be – 10th Anniversary Edition* (New York: William Morrow, 2005, 2015), 194–195.

55 "Origins," Downtown CREDO, accessed November 25, 2022, http://www.downtowncredo.com/story.

56 Megan Hexum, "Ben Hoyer," Campuspeak, accessed November 25, 2022, https://campuspeak.com/speaker/ben-hoyer/.

57 Dean Caravelis, "Ben Hoyer," *Outrageously Remarkable* (blog), May 9, 2017, https://deancaravelis.com/ben-hoyer.

58 Steve Blount et al., "Hearts of Gold," *Orlando: The City's Magazine,* January 3, 2011, http://www.orlandomagazine.com/Orlando-Magazine/January-2011/Hearts-of-Gold.

59  Natalie Orenstein, "Building Health Organically in a Small Florida Community," Build Healthy Places Network, May 20, 2016, http://www.buildhealthyplaces.org/whats-new/building-health-organically-small-florida-community.

60  Luke 12:48, second half (New International Version).

61  Erica Pender et al., "Trustworthiness, Trust and Influence in Organizational Decision Making," Conference paper presented at the European Association of Work and Organizational Psychology Conference, May 2015, https://doi.org/10.13140/RG.2.1.3631.7205.

62  Bennet Omalu et al., "Chronic Traumatic Encephalopathy in a National Football League Player," *Neurosurgery* 57, no. 1 (July 2005): 128–34, https://www.ncbi.nlm.nih.gov/pubmed/15987548.

63  Bennet Omalu, "The Doctor Who Discovered the Dangers of Concussions in Football," *Guideposts*, September 2017, https://www.guideposts.org/better-living/life-advice/finding-life-purpose/the-doctor-who-discovered-the-dangers-of-concussions.

64  1 Corinthians 15:33 (New International Version).

65  Robyn Shapiro et al., "A Survey of Sued and Nonsued Physicians and Suing Patients," *Archives of Internal Medicine* 149, no. 10 (October 1, 1989): 2190–2196, https://doi.org/10.1001/archinte.1989.00390100028008.

66  Peter F. Drucker, "Peter Drucker: Father of Modern Management," *A World of Ideas*, interview with Bill Moyer, November 17, 1988, https://billmoyers.com/content/peter-drucker/.

67  "The UGLI Orange Exercise," adapted from George Mason University Institute for Conflict Analysis and Resolution, accessed November 25, 2022, http://jfmueller.faculty.noctrl.edu/crow/ugliorangesactivity.pdf.

68  Catherine Rothon et al., "Physical Activity and Depressive Symptoms in Adolescents: A Prospective Study," *BMC Medicine* 8 (May 28, 2010): 32, https://doi.org/10.1186/1741-7015-8-32.

69  Ariel Shensa et al., "Social Media Use and Depression and Anxiety Symptoms: A Cluster Analysis," *American Journal of Health Behavior* 42, no. 2 (March 1, 2018): 116–128, https://doi.org/10.5993/AJHB.42.2.11.

70  "Loneliness Statistics 2022: Demographics, USA & Worldwide," Social Self, accessed November 25, 2022, https://socialself.com/loneliness-statistics/#1.

71  Allison Sadlier, "1 in 4 Americans Say They Have No One to Confide in," SWNS digital, accessed November 25, https://swnsdigital.com/us/2019/04/1-in-4-americans-say-they-have-no-one-to-confide-in/.

72  Joe Pinsker, "The Hidden Costs of Living Alone," *The Atlantic,* October 20, 2021, https://www.theatlantic.com/family/archive/2021/10/living-alone-couple-partner-single/620434/.

73  Ye Li et al., "Dietary Patterns and Depression Risk: A Meta-Analysis," *Psychiatry Research* 253 (July 2017): 373–382, https://doi.org/10.1016/j.psychres.2017.04.020.

74  Clear, *Atomic Habits,* 53–54.

75  Harold G. Koenig, *Medicine, Religion, and Health: Where Science and Spirituality Meet* (West Conshohocken, PA: Templeton Foundation Press, 2008), 53.

76  Denise Cooper, Julian Thayer, and Shari Waldstein, "Coping with Racism: The Impact of Prayer on Cardiovascular Reactivity and Post-Stress Recovery in African American Women," *Annals of Behavioral Medicine* 47, no. 2 (April 2014): 218–230, https://doi.org/10.1007/s12160-013-9540-4.

77  Simin Hematti et al., "Spiritual Well-Being for Increasing Life Expectancy in Palliative Radiotherapy Patients: A Question-

naire-Based Study," *Journal of Religious Health* 54, no. 5 (October 2015): 1563–1572, https://doi.org/ 10.1007/s10943-014-9872-9.

78  Renate Ysseldyk, S. Alexander Haslam, and Catherine Haslam, "Abide with Me: Religious Group Identification among Older Adults Promotes Health and Well-Being by Maintaining Multiple Group Memberships," *Aging & Mental Health* 17, no. 7 (April 2013): 869–879, http://dx.doi.org/10.1080/13607863.2013.799120.

79  James W. Anderson and Paige Nunnelley, "Private Prayer Associations with Depression, Anxiety and Other Health Conditions: An Analytical Review of Clinical Studies," *Postgraduate Medicine* 128, no. 7 (July 22, 2016): 635–641, https://doi.org/10.1080/0032548 1.2016.1209962.

80  Stephen Ganocy et al., "Association of Spirituality with Mental Health Conditions in Ohio National Guard Soldiers," *The Journal of Nervous and Mental Disease* 204, no. 7 (April 2016): 524–529, https://doi.org/ 10.1097/NMD.0000000000000519.

81  Hematti et al., "Spiritual Well-Being for Increasing Life Expectancy in Palliative Radiotherapy Patients," 1563–1572.

82  Naomi T. Tabak and Amy Weisman de Mamani, "Religion's Effect on Mental Health in Schizophrenia: Examining the Roles of Meaning-Making and Seeking Social Support," *Clinical Schizophrenia and Related Psychoses* 8, no. 2 (July 1, 2014): 91–100, https://doi.org/10.3371/CSRP.TUWE.021513.

83  Evangelos Fradelos et al., "Integrating Chronic Kidney Disease Patient's Spirituality in Their Care: Health Benefits and Research Perspectives," *Materia Socio-Medica* 27, no. 5 (October 2015): 354–358, https://doi.org/10.5455/msm.2015.27.354-358.

84  David L. Roth et al., "Religious Involvement and Health Over Time: Predictive Effects in a National Sample of African Americans," *Journal for the Scientific Study of Religion* 55, no. 2 (June 2016): 417–424, https://doi.org/10.1111/jssr.12269.

85  Viktor E. Frankl, *Man's Search for Meaning: An Introduction to Logotherapy* (New York: Beacon Press, 2006).

86  Neel Burton, "Man's Search for Meaning: Meaning as a Cure for Depression and Other Ills," *Psychology Today*, revised May 4, 2020, https://www.psychologytoday.com/blog/hide-and-seek/201205/mans-search-meaning.

87  Martin Seligman, *Flourish: A Visionary New Understanding of Happiness and Well-Being* (New York: Free Press, 2011), 12.

88  Thomas Seager, "Pursue Meaning, Not Happiness," Self-Actual Engineering, accessed November 25, 2022, https://seagertp.substack.com/p/pursue-meaning-not-happiness.

89  Emily Esfahani Smith, "There's More to Life Than Being Happy," filmed April 2017, TED Talk video, 12:18, https://www.ted.com/talks/emily_esfahani_smith_there_s_more_to_life_than_being_happy.

90  Harold Koenig, *The Healing Power of Faith: Science Explores Medicine's Last Great Frontier* (New York: Simon & Schuster, 1999), 24.

91  Jeffrey Levin, Linda Chatters, and Robert Joseph Taylor, "Religious Effects on Health Status and Life Satisfaction Among Black Americans," *Journal of Gerontology B: Social Sciences* 50, no. 3 (May 1995): S154–63.

92  Christina Puchalski, "The Role of Spirituality in Healthcare," *Baylor University Medical Center Proceedings* 14, no. 4 (October 14, 2001): 352–357, https://www.ncbi.nlm.nih.gov/pmc/articles/PMC1305900/.

93  Corrine McLaughlin, "Spirituality and Ethics in Business," *European Business Review* 17, no. 1 (2005), https://doi.org/10.1108/ebr.2005.05417aab.004.

94  Clay Routledge, "5 Scientifically Supported Benefits of Prayer," *Psychology Today*, posted June 23, 2014, accessed February 14, 2018, https://www.psychologytoday.com/blog/more-mortal/201406/5-scientifically-supported-benefits-prayer.

95  *Oxford Learner's Dictionaries*, s.v. "self-reflection," accessed November 28, 2022, https://www.oxfordlearnersdictionaries.com/definition/english/self-reflection?q=self-reflection.

96  Emmett Martin and Laura A. Warner, "Using Commitment as a Tool to Promote Behavior Change in Extension Programming," *The Journal of Extension* 53, no. 4 (August 2015): Article 32, https://archives.joe.org/joe/2015august/tt4.php.

97  Doug McKenzie-Mohr and P. Wesley Schultz, "Choosing Effective Behavior Change Tools." *Social Marketing Quarterly* 20, no. 1 (January 2014): 35–46, https://doi.org/10.1177/1524500413519257.

98  Chin Ming Hui and Daniel Molden, "Maintaining Commitment in the Presence of Alternative Opportunities: The Role of Motivations for Prevention or Promotion," *Social Cognition* 32, no. 6 (December 2014): 571–584, https://doi.org/10.1521/soco.2014.32.6.571.

# A free ebook edition is available with the purchase of this book.

**To claim your free ebook edition:**

1. Visit MorganJamesBOGO.com
2. Sign your name CLEARLY in the space
3. Complete the form and submit a photo of the entire copyright page
4. You or your friend can download the ebook to your preferred device

A **FREE** ebook edition is available for you or a friend with the purchase of this print book.

CLEARLY SIGN YOUR NAME ABOVE

**Instructions to claim your free ebook edition:**
1. Visit MorganJamesBOGO.com
2. Sign your name CLEARLY in the space above
3. Complete the form and submit a photo of this entire page
4. You or your friend can download the ebook to your preferred device

## Print & Digital Together Forever.

Snap a photo

Free ebook

Read anywhere